Predictive Analytics Using Rattle and Qlik Sense

Create comprehensive solutions for predictive analysis
using Rattle and share them with Qlik Sense

Ferran Garcia Pagans

PUBLISHING

BIRMINGHAM - MUMBAI

Predictive Analytics Using Rattle and Qlik Sense

First published: June 2015

Production reference: 1260615

Published by Packt Publishing Ltd.
Livery Place
35 Livery Street
Birmingham B3 2PB, UK.

ISBN 978-1-78439-580-3

www.packtpub.com

Credits

Author
Ferran Garcia Pagans

Reviewers
Gert Jan Feick

Miguel Ángel García

Commissioning Editor
Dipika Gaonkar

Acquisition Editor
Reshma Raman

Content Development Editor
Ajinkya Paranjape

Technical Editor
Narsimha Pai

Copy Editors
Janbal Dharmaraj

Brandt D'Mello

Kevin McGowan

Aditya Nair

Rashmi Sawant

Project Coordinator
Harshal Ved

Proofreader
Safis Editing

Indexer
Hemangini Bari

Graphics
Sheetal Aute

Production Coordinator
Komal Ramchandani

Cover Work
Komal Ramchandani

About the Author

Ferran Garcia Pagans studied software engineering at the University of Girona and Ramon Llull University. After that, he did his masters in business administration at ESADE Business School. He has 16 years of experience in the software industry, where he helped customers from different industries to create software solutions. He started his career working at the Ramon Llull University as a teacher and researcher. Then, he moved to the Volkswagen group as a software developer. After that, he worked with Oracle as a Java, SOA, and BPM specialist. Currently, he is a solution architect at Qlik, where he helps customers to achieve competitive advantages with data applications.

I would like to thank my love, Laura.

About the Reviewers

Gert Jan Feick studied informatics (language, knowledge, and interaction) at Technical University Enschede (NL). He started his career as a project manager at a medium-sized software development company, specializing in requirement analysis and project management. From 2005 onward, he was responsible for building up a company in the areas of software development, reporting and visualizations, and analysis. In 2011, he moved to Germany and became a management consultant at Infomotion GmbH, where he was responsible for the team that works on self-service and Agile BI as well as reporting and analysis.

He regularly contributes to online forums (including the Qlik Community), speaks at conventions, and writes articles. You can follow him on Twitter at @gjfeick, where he tweets about QlikView, big data, self-service and Agile BI, data visualization, and other topics in general.

Miguel Ángel García is a Business Intelligence consultant and QlikView Solutions Architect. Having worked throughout many successful QlikView implementations, from inception through implementation, and performed across a wide variety of roles on each project; his experience and skills range from presales to applications development and design, technical architecture, system administration, functional analysis, and overall project execution.

He is the co-author of *QlikView 11 for Developers*, *Packt Publishing*, which was published in November 2012, and its corresponding translation into Spanish "QlikView 11 para Desarrolladores", published in December 2013. He also worked as a technical reviewer for several other QlikView books.

He runs a QlikView consultancy, AfterSync (www.aftersync.com), through which he helps customers discover the power of the Qlik platform.

He currently holds the QlikView Designer, QlikView Developer, and QlikView System Administrator certifications, issued by Qlik, for Versions 9, 10, and 11.

www.PacktPub.com

Support files, eBooks, discount offers, and more

For support files and downloads related to your book, please visit www.PacktPub.com.

Did you know that Packt offers eBook versions of every book published, with PDF and ePub files available? You can upgrade to the eBook version at www.PacktPub.com and as a print book customer, you are entitled to a discount on the eBook copy. Get in touch with us at service@packtpub.com for more details.

At www.PacktPub.com, you can also read a collection of free technical articles, sign up for a range of free newsletters and receive exclusive discounts and offers on Packt books and eBooks.

https://www2.packtpub.com/books/subscription/packtlib

Do you need instant solutions to your IT questions? PacktLib is Packt's online digital book library. Here, you can search, access, and read Packt's entire library of books.

Why subscribe?

- Fully searchable across every book published by Packt
- Copy and paste, print, and bookmark content
- On demand and accessible via a web browser

Free access for Packt account holders

If you have an account with Packt at www.PacktPub.com, you can use this to access PacktLib today and view 9 entirely free books. Simply use your login credentials for immediate access.

Instant updates on new Packt books

Get notified! Find out when new books are published by following @PacktEnterprise on Twitter or the *Packt Enterprise* Facebook page.

Table of Contents

Preface

Today, a lot of organizations are investing in improving their analytics skills and tools. They know that, by analyzing their data, they can improve the performance of their business process and achieve real value from that.

The objective of this book is to introduce you to predictive analytics and data visualization by developing some example applications. We'll use R and Rattle to create the predictive model and Qlik Sense to create a data application that allows business users to explore their data.

We use Rattle and Qlik Sense to avoid learn programming and focus on predictive analytics and data visualizations concepts.

What this book covers

Chapter 1, *Getting Ready with Predictive Analytics*, explains the key concepts of predictive analytics and how to install our learning environments, such as Qlik Sense, R, and Rattle.

Chapter 2, *Preparing Your Data*, covers the basic characteristics of datasets, how to load a dataset into Rattle, and how to transform it. As data is the basic ingredient of analytics, preparing the data to analyze it is the first step.

Chapter 3, *Exploring and Understanding Your Data*, introduces you to Exploratory Data Analysis (EDA) using Rattle. EDA is a statistical approach to understanding data.

Chapter 4, *Creating Your First Qlik Sense Application*, discusses how to load a dataset into Qlik Sense, create a data model and basic charts, and explore data using Qlik Sense. Using Exploratory Data Analysis and Rattle to understand our data is a very mathematical approach. Usually, business users prefer a more intuitive approach, such as Qlik Sense

Chapter 5, Clustering and Other Unsupervised Learning Methods, covers machine, supervised, and unsupervised learning but focuses on unsupervised learning We create an example application using K-means, a classic machine learning algorithm. We use Rattle to process the dataset and then we load it into Qlik Sense to present the data to the business user.

Chapter 6, Decision Trees and Other Supervised Learning Methods, focuses on supervised learning. It helps you create an example application using Decision Tree Learning. We use Rattle to process the data and Qlik Sense to communicate with it.

Chapter 7, Model Evaluation, explains how to evaluate the performance of a model. Model evaluation is very useful to improve the performance.

Chapter 8, Visualizations, Data Applications, Dashboards, and Data Storytelling, focuses on data visualization and data storytelling using Qlik Sense.

Chapter 9, Developing a Complete Application, explains how to create a complete application. It covers how to explore the data, create a predictive model, and create a data application.

What you need for this book

To install our learning environment and complete the examples, you need a 64-bit computer:

- OS: Windows 7, Windows 8, or 8.1
- Processor: Intel Core2 Duo or higher
- Memory: 4 GB or more
- .NET Framework: 4.0
- Security: Local admin privileges to install R, Rattle, and Qlik Sense.

Who this book is for

If you are a business analyst who wants to understand how to improve your data analysis and how to apply predictive analytics, then this book is ideal for you. This book assumes that you to have some basic knowledge of QlikView, but no knowledge of implementing predictive analysis with QlikView. It would also be helpful to be familiar with the basic concepts of statistics and a spreadsheet editor, such as Excel.

Conventions

In this book, you will find a number of text styles that distinguish between different kinds of information. Here are some examples of these styles and an explanation of their meaning.

Code words in text, database table names, folder names, filenames, file extensions, pathnames, dummy URLs, user input, and Twitter handles are shown as follows: "After you have downloaded it, type `library(rattle)` and R will load the Rattle package into memory, and you will be able to use it."

A block of code is set as follows:

```
If Purpose = 'Education' AND Sex = 'male' AND Age > 25 Then No
Default
If Purpose = 'Education' AND Sex = 'male' AND Age < 25 Then Yes
Default
```

New terms and **important words** are shown in bold. Words that you see on the screen, for example, in menus or dialog boxes, appear in the text like this: "Don't be afraid, we will use two software tools Rattle and **Qlik Sense Desktop** in order to avoid complex code."

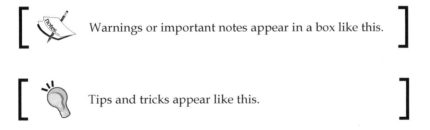

Warnings or important notes appear in a box like this.

Tips and tricks appear like this.

Reader feedback

Feedback from our readers is always welcome. Let us know what you think about this book—what you liked or disliked. Reader feedback is important for us as it helps us develop titles that you will really get the most out of.

To send us general feedback, simply e-mail `feedback@packtpub.com`, and mention the book's title in the subject of your message.

If there is a topic that you have expertise in and you are interested in either writing or contributing to a book, see our author guide at `www.packtpub.com/authors`.

Customer support

Now that you are the proud owner of a Packt book, we have a number of things to help you to get the most from your purchase.

Downloading the example code

You can download the example code files from your account at `http://www.packtpub.com` for all the Packt Publishing books you have purchased. If you purchased this book elsewhere, you can visit `http://www.packtpub.com/support` and register to have the files e-mailed directly to you.

Downloading the color images of this book

We also provide you with a PDF file that has color images of the screenshots/diagrams used in this book. The color images will help you better understand the changes in the output. You can download this file from `http://www.packtpub.com/sites/default/files/downloads/5803EN_ColorImages.pdf`.

Errata

Although we have taken every care to ensure the accuracy of our content, mistakes do happen. If you find a mistake in one of our books — maybe a mistake in the text or the code — we would be grateful if you could report this to us. By doing so, you can save other readers from frustration and help us improve subsequent versions of this book. If you find any errata, please report them by visiting `http://www.packtpub.com/submit-errata`, selecting your book, clicking on the **Errata Submission Form** link, and entering the details of your errata. Once your errata are verified, your submission will be accepted and the errata will be uploaded to our website or added to any list of existing errata under the Errata section of that title.

To view the previously submitted errata, go to `https://www.packtpub.com/books/content/support` and enter the name of the book in the search field. The required information will appear under the **Errata** section.

Piracy

Piracy of copyrighted material on the Internet is an ongoing problem across all media. At Packt, we take the protection of our copyright and licenses very seriously. If you come across any illegal copies of our works in any form on the Internet, please provide us with the location address or website name immediately so that we can pursue a remedy.

Please contact us at `copyright@packtpub.com` with a link to the suspected pirated material.

We appreciate your help in protecting our authors and our ability to bring you valuable content.

Questions

If you have a problem with any aspect of this book, you can contact us at `questions@packtpub.com`, and we will do our best to address the problem.

1
Getting Ready with Predictive Analytics

Analytics, predictive analytics, and data visualization are trendy topics today. The reasons are:

- Today a lot of internal and external data is available
- Technology to use this data has evolved a lot
- It is commonly accepted that there is a lot of value that can be extracted from data

As in many trendy topics, there is a lot of confusion around it. In this chapter, we will cover the following concepts:

- Introducing the key concepts of the book and tools we're going to use
- Defining analytics, predictive analytics, and data visualization
- Explaining the purpose of this book and the methodology we'll follow
- Covering the installation of the environment we'll use to create examples of applications in each chapter

After this chapter, we'll learn how to use our data to make predictions that will add value to our organizations. Before starting a data project, you always need to understand how your project will add value to the organization. In an analytics project, the two main sources of value are cost reduction and revenue increase. When you're working on a fraud detection project, your objective is to reduce fraud; this will lead into a cost reduction that will improve the margin of the organization. Finally, to understand the value of your data solution, you need to evaluate the cost of your solution. The real value added to an organization is the difference between the provided value and the total cost.

Working with data to create predictive solutions sounds very glamorous, but before that we'll learn how to use Rattle to load data, to avoid some problems related to the quality of the data, and to explore it. Rattle is a tool for statisticians, and, sometimes, we need a tool that provides us with a business approach to data exploration. We'll learn how to use Qlik Sense Desktop to do this.

After learning how to explore and understand data, we'll now learn how to create predictive systems. We'll divide these systems into unsupervised learning methods and supervised learning methods. We'll explain the difference later in this book.

To achieve a better understanding, in this book we'll create three different solutions using the most common predictive techniques: Clustering, Decision Trees, and Linear Regression.

To present data to the user, we need to create an application that helps the user to understand the data and take decisions; for this reason we'll look at the basics of data visualization. Data Visualization, Predictive Analytics and most of the topics of this book are huge knowledge areas. In this book we'll introduce you to these topics and at the end of each chapter you will find a section called *Further learning* where you will find references to continue learning.

Analytics, predictive analytics, and data visualization

In January 2006, Thomas H. Davenport, a well-known American academic author, published an article in *Harvard Business Review* called *Competing on Analytics*. In this article, the author explains the need for analytics in this way:

> *"Organizations are competing on analytics not just because they can — business today is awash in data and data crunchers — but also because they should. At a time when firms in many industries offer similar products and use comparable technologies, business processes are among the last remaining points of differentiation. And analytics competitors wring every last drop of value from those processes."*

After this article, companies in different industries started to learn how to use traditional and new data sources to gain competitive advantages; but what is analytics?

Today, the term analytics is used to describe different techniques and methods that extract new knowledge from data and communicate it. The term comprises statistics, data mining, machine learning, operations research, data visualization, and many other areas.

An important point is that analytics will not provide any new value or advantage by itself; it will help people to take better decisions. **Analytics** is about replacing decisions based on feelings and intuition with decisions based on data and evidence.

Predictive analytics is a subset of analytics whose objective is to extract knowledge from data and use it to predict something. Eric Siegel in his book *Predictive Analytics* describes the term as:

> "*Technology that learns from experience (data) to predict the future behavior of individuals in order to drive better decisions.*"

Generally, in real life, an accurate prediction is not possible, but we can extract a lot of value from predictions with low accuracy. Think of an insurance company, they have a lot of claims to review, but have just a few people to do it. They know that some claims are fraudulent, but they don't have enough people and time to review all claims. They can randomly choose some claims or they can develop a system that selects the claims with a higher probability of fraud. If their system predictions are better than just guessing, they will improve their fraud detecting efforts and they will save a lot of money in fraudulent claims.

As we've seen, everything is about helping people to take better decisions; for this reason we've got to communicate the insights we've discovered from data in an easy to understand and intuitive way, especially when we deal with complex problems. **Data visualization** can help us to communicate our discoveries to our users. The term, data visualization, is used in many disciplines with many different meanings. We use this term to describe the visual representation of data; our main goal is to communicate information clearly and efficiently to business users.

In this introduction, we've used the term *value* many times and it's important to have an intuitive definition. We develop software solutions to obtain a business benefit; generally, we want to increase income or reduce cost. This business benefit has an economic value; the difference between this economic value and the cost of developing the solution is the value you will obtain.

Usually, a predictive analytics project follows some common steps that we call the predictive analytics process:

1. **Problem definition**: Before we start, we need to understand the business problem and the goals.

2. **Extract and load data**: An analytics application starts with raw data that is stored in a database, files, or other systems. We need to extract data from its original location and load it into our analytics tools.

3. **Prepare data**: Sometimes, the data needs transformation because of its format or because of poor quality.

4. **Create a model**: In this step, we will develop the predictive model.

5. **Performance evaluation**: After creating the model, we'll evaluate its performance.

6. **Deploy the model and create a visual application**: In the last step, we will deploy the predictive model and create the application for the business user.

The steps in this process don't have strict borders; sometimes, we go back and forth in the process.

Purpose of the book

This is not a technical guide about R and Qlik Sense integration, or a Rattle guide for software developers. This book is an introduction to the basic techniques of predictive analytics and data visualization. We've written this book for business analysts, and people with an IT background, but without analytics experience.

"Tell me and I forget, teach me and I may remember, involve me and I learn."

– Benjamin Franklin

We believe that the best way to learn is by practicing, and for this reason this book is organized around examples, which you can do with a simple Windows computer. Don't be afraid, we will use two software tools, Rattle and Qlik Sense Desktop, in order to avoid complex code. To create the predictive analysis, we'll use *Rattle* and for data visualization, we'll use *Qlik Sense Desktop.*

There are two ways of using Rattle, or R, and Qlik Sense Desktop together. These are listed as follows:

- In the first approach, it is possible to integrate Qlik Sense Desktop and R. The business users select some data. Qlik Sense Desktop sends this selected data to an R server, the server processes the data and performs a prediction. The R server returns the data to Qlik Sense Desktop, and this shows the data to the user. This model has a great advantage—the interactivity, but it also has a disadvantage; it requires additional software to integrate the two different environments.

- The second approach is based on two steps. In the first step, the R environment loads the data, performs the prediction, and stores the original data with the prediction. In the second step, Qlik Sense Desktop loads the data and the prediction, and shows it to the business user. This second approach has a great advantage which is simplicity, but also has a disadvantage which is the lack of interactivity.

In this book, we'll use the second approach because in predictive analytics choosing the appropriate model is the key. For this reason we want to focus on introducing you to different models, avoiding the technical stuff of integration. We'll use Rattle and Qlik Sense Desktop in a two-step process. We'll load data in Rattle to enrich it with a predictive model and then load it in Qlik Sense Desktop to share it by creating data visualizations. This process is illustrated in the following diagram:

Introducing R, Rattle, and Qlik Sense Desktop

In this section, we will introduce the tools we'll use in this book: R, Rattle, and Qlik Sense Desktop.

R is a free programming language for statistics and graphics available under the terms of the Free Software Foundation's **General Public License (GNU)**. The R language is widely accepted for statistical analysis and data mining. There is a big community of developers that develop new packages for R, such as Rattle.

R is a very powerful and flexible programming language, but to create predictive models with R you need to be a skilled programmer. For this reason, we will use Rattle.

Rattle is a **Graphical User Interface (GUI)** for data mining developed by Graham Williamson using R. Similar to R, Rattle is also licensed under the GNU. R and Rattle are the predictive analysis environments that we will be using in this book.

Using Rattle, we'll be able to load and prepare data, create a predictive model, and evaluate its performance without writing R code; Rattle will write the code for us.

In order to create a visual and intuitive application for the business user, we'll use Qlik Sense Desktop, the personal and free version of Qlik Sense. Qlik Sense is a self-service data visualization tool developed by Qlik.

We'll use Qlik Sense Desktop instead of Qlik Sense Enterprise because we want to build a free learning environment to develop the examples of this book. For the propose of this book, Qlik Sense Desktop and Qlik Sense are very similar. When you deploy your applications in Qlik Sense Enterprise, the platform provides you:

- Data governance.
- Security
- Scalability
- High availability

Qlik has two different tools for data analysis and data visualization: QlikView and Qlik Sense. Each tool is designed to solve a different problem:

- With QlikView, developers have a powerful tool to create guided analytic applications
- With Qlik Sense, business users can create their own analysis and visualizations with drag and drop simplicity

We will use Qlik Sense Desktop instead of QlikView because the book is written for business users and analysts, and Qlik Sense is designed to provide business users with the ability to create visualizations on their data.

- Qlik Sense has two different editions:
- Qlik Sense Enterprise, a sever based edition for use in organizations.
- Qlik Sense Desktop, a desktop edition for personal use.
- In this book we'll use Qlik Sense Desktop to complete the examples. This edition is free for personal utilization.

R and Rattle can be installed on Windows, Mac OS, and Linux, but Qlik Sense Desktop can only be installed on a Windows machine. For this reason, we will use a Windows-based computer for this book. Qlik Sense Desktop and R load all data into memory; we suggest that you use a 64-bit computer instead of a 32-bit computer.

In order to install R, Rattle, and Qlik Sense Desktop, you'll need administration rights, and an Internet connection to download the software.

Installing the environment

In the examples, we'll use Rattle and Qlik Sense Desktop, but, as we've explained, Rattle is an R package and we need to install R too. We will follow these steps:

1. Download and install R.
2. Download and install Rattle.
3. Download and install Qlik Sense Desktop.

Downloading and installing R

These steps must be followed for installing R:

1. Go to the homepage of **R Project for Statistical Computing** at `www.r-project.org`.

2. In the navigation bar, click on **Comprehensive R Archive Network (CRAN)** and you will be redirected to a list of CRAN mirrors. Choose a download mirror that is the closest to your geographic location, as shown here:

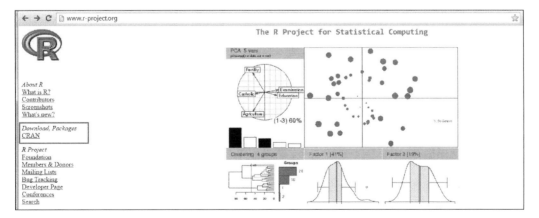

3. You will reach a different page; choose **Download R for Windows**, and in the following page click on **install R for the first time**.

4. Finally, you will reach the download page. As of writing this book, the latest version for Windows was 3.1.2. Click on **Download R 3.1.2 for Windows** to download the installation program, as shown in this screenshot:

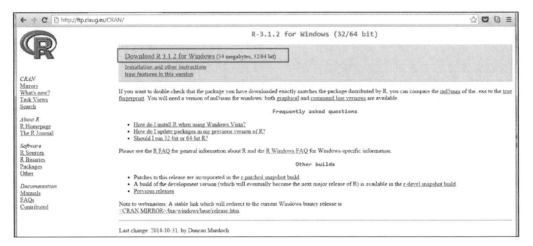

5. Run the installation program, `R-3.1.2-win.exe`, to start the process. Depending on the level of security of your system, it will ask you for permission to execute the program and to make modifications on your system. You have to allow this to start the process.

6. In the next step, you have to choose a language; choose **English**. For the rest of the installation process, leave the default options.

7. When the installation process finishes, you will have two new icons on your desktop— **R i386 3.1.2** and **R x64 3.1.2**; use the first one if you are using a 32-bit computer and the second one if you are using a 64-bit computer:

Starting the R Console to test your R installation

The **R Console** is a window used to interact with R language; you can type commands and functions here, and you will see the results in the same window. We will not focus on R, so we'll only learn the commands needed to work with Rattle.

The following steps are needed to start and close **R Console**:

1. Double-click the R icon to start the **R Console**.

2. To exit the **R Console**, type q() and press *Enter*, as shown here:

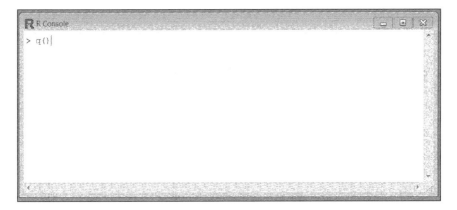

Downloading and installing Rattle

Rattle is an R package, which is a collection of functions and data someone else has developed, and we can use it in our programs. If you already have some hands-on experience with R, then this task should be a much lighter task.

Before starting with the installation, remember that you need an active Internet connection. The following are the steps to install Rattle:

1. We will install Rattle from **R Console**; to open it double-click on the **R x64 3.1.1** desktop icon.

2. In **R Console**, type `install.packages("rattle")` and press *Enter*. The **R Console** will show you a list of **CRAN** mirrors; choose a download mirror that is the closest to your geographic location and R will download the Rattle package, as shown here:

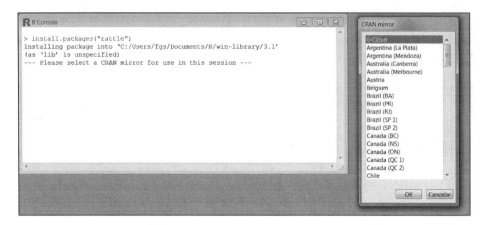

3. After you have downloaded it, type `library(rattle)` and R will load the Rattle package into memory, and you will be able to use it. Use the `rattle()` command to start Rattle:

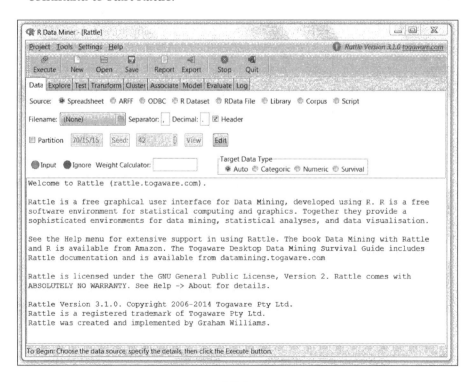

Rattle needs other R packages to work properly, the first time you open Rattle, the system will ask your permission to install some packages; in order to execute Rattle, you have to accept the installation of these packages.

4. To exit, click on the **Quit** icon from Rattle GUI and type `q()` in the **R Console**:

 If you are from a non-English speaking country, you've probably installed everything in English, but Rattle's texts appear in your own language. Rattle will work fine in your language, but this book is written in English and it will refer to Rattle's functions and menus using English names. If you prefer to execute Rattle in English, quit Rattle and type `Sys.setenv(LANGUAGE="en")` in your **R Console** and start Rattle again.

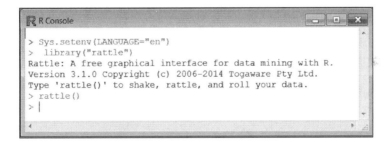

 Rattle's menu now appears in English.

Installing Qlik Sense Desktop

In order to install **Qlik Sense Desktop**, you need a 64-bit computer with the following specifications:

- Windows 7 or Windows 8.x
- Administrator privileges

- .NET Framework 4.0
- 4 GB of RAM memory
- 500 MB of disk space
- Intel Core 2 Duo processor or higher

Probably, you are not sure if you have .NET Framework on your computer; don't worry if you don't have it, the installer will offer to install it.

The following steps are used to install **Qlik Sense Desktop**:

1. Go to the Qlik home page, `http://www.qlik.com`. Click on the **Free Downloads** link in the upper-right corner. The following page will open:

2. Click on the **Get Qlik Sense Desktop** button to download **Qlik Sense Desktop**.
3. When the download finishes, execute the installation program by double-clicking the file you've downloaded:

Name	Date modified	Type	Size
Qlik_Sense_Desktop_setup	25/07/2014 15:16	Application	122.563 KB

4. The installation process is very easy; you just need to click on **INSTALL** when **Qlik Sense Desktop installer** starts and accept the license agreement:

 In case the installer prompts to install .NET Framework 4.0 (if you haven't already done so), then follow the onscreen instructions to install it.

5. When the installer finishes, click on **Finish** to exit the installation program. You'll find a new **Qlik Sense Desktop** icon on your desktop.

 Keep the installation program in a safe directory on your hard disk. You can use it to repair your installation if something happens and to uninstall **Qlik Sense Desktop**.

Exploring Qlik Sense Desktop

In this section, we will get a first taste of **Qlik Sense Desktop**. We will open it and do a quick exploration. After installing it, **Qlik Sense Desktop** has three example applications **Executive Dashboard**, **Helpdesk Management**, and **Sales Discovery**. We will explore the **Executive Dashboard** application.

Follow these steps to explore **Qlik Sense Desktop**:

1. Open **Qlik Sense Desktop** by double-clicking the **Qlik Sense Desktop** icon on the desktop:

2. When **Qlik Sense Desktop** opens, click on the cross (highlighted in the following screenshot) in the central window to close the startup dialog:

Now, you are in the **Qlik Sense Desktop** hub, the main screen of **Qlik Sense Desktop**. From this screen, the user can open, access, and manage his applications. We've highlighted four different areas in the hub's screen:

* In area **1**, you can find the help section.

* Area **2** is the main section of this screen. In this section, the users have their applications. As you already know, **Qlik Sense Desktop** comes with three demo applications.

- ° In area **3**, there is a button to create a new application and two buttons to manage the layout.
- ° In area **4**, you have a button to access QlikCloud and a search button, as shown here:

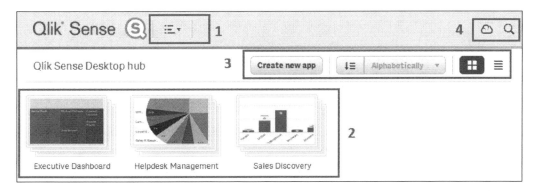

3. We'll explore an application. Click on the **Executive Dashboard** button to open it.

4. A Qlik Sense application is organized in different sheets, such as a spreadsheet. This application contains three sheets, and you can always create a new sheet by clicking in the **Create new sheet** button, which is visible in the following screenshot:

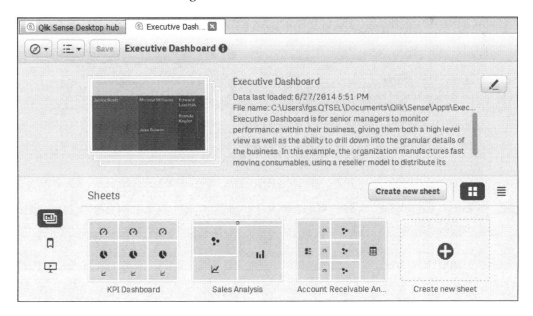

5. Click on the **KPI Dashboard** icon to open this sheet. This sheet shows three **Key Performance Indicators (KPI)** — **Expenses**, **Revenue vs Last year**, and **Account Receivables**. For each KPI, we see the current level, a distribution, and temporal evolution. At the left-hand side, there are three filters — **Product**, **Segment**, and **Customer**:

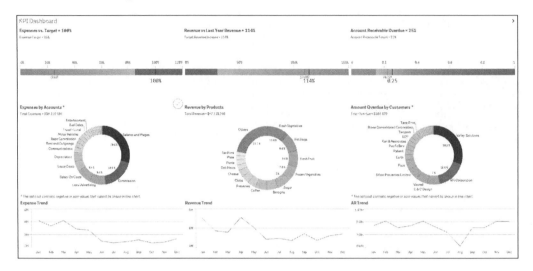

6. Using the button located in the top-right corner, you can toggle between the sheets. Go to the **Sales Analysis** sheet:

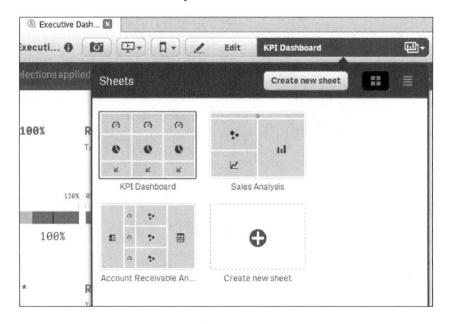

7. The **Sales Analysis** sheet has four filters in the top area: **Segment**, **Region**, **Sales Rep Name**, and **Product Group**:

8. Click on the **Region** filter and select **Europe**; the dashboard will react to show only the data related to **Europe**. Confirm your selection by clicking the highlighted tick icon:

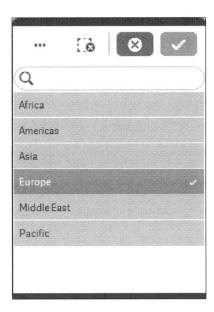

9. Qlik Sense keeps your selection in the top-left side of the screen. You can delete these filters by clicking on the cross (highlighted in the following screenshot):

10. We'll come back to Qlik Sense in *Chapter 4, Creating Your First Qlik Sense Application*; now close the window to exit **Qlik Sense Desktop**.

Further learning

In August 2006, after his famous article, *Thomas H. Davenport* and *Jeanne G. Harris* published a book about the same idea:

Competing on Analytics: The New Science of Winning, by Thomas H. Davenport and Jeanne G. Harris, *Harvard Business School Press*.

A good place to understand all the power of predictive analytics is the book by Eric Siegel. This book contains 147 examples of predictive analytics in its central pages:

Predictive Analytics: the power to predict who will click, buy, lie or die, Eric Siegel, John Wiley & Sons, Inc.

We will not cover R Language in this book. If you want to learn how to program in R, I recommend that you read the following book:

Statistical Analysis with R, John M. Quick, Packt Publishing.

We'll come back to **Qlik Sense Desktop** in *Chapter 4, Creating Your First Qlik Sense Application*. If you want to be more familiar with Qlik Sense, you can start here `www.qlik.com/en-US/sense/gettingstarted`.

Summary

In this chapter, we've introduced analytics as a process that starts with raw data and creates new knowledge to help people to take better decisions.

We also defined predictive analytics as a process that learns to create predictions from the data. Finally, we've defined data visualization as a technology that will help us to communicate data-based knowledge more efficiently.

After introducing the key concepts of the book, we've also described R, Rattle, and Qlik Sense, the tools we'll use to build the examples. And finally, we've installed the environment.

In *Chapter 2, Handling Docker Containers*, we'll explain how to load data into Rattle and how we can use Rattle to transform it.

2
Preparing Your Data

The French term *mise en place* is used in professional kitchens to describe the practice of chefs organizing and arranging the ingredients up to a point where it is ready to be used. It may be as simple as washing and picking herbs into individual leaves or chopping vegetables, or as complicated as caramelizing onions or slow cooking meats.

In the same way, before we start cooking the data or building a predictive model, we need to prepare the ingredients-the data. Our preparation covers three different tasks:

- Loading the data into the analytic tool
- Exploring the data to understand it and to find quality problems with it
- Transforming the data to fix the quality problems

We say that the quality of data is high when it's appropriate for a specific use. In this chapter, we'll describe characteristics of data related to its quality.

As we've seen, our *mise en place* has three steps. After loading the data, we need to explore it and transform it. Exploring and transforming is an iterative process, but in this book, we'll divide it in two different steps for clarity.

In this chapter, we'll discuss the following topics:

- Datasets and types of variables
- Data quality
- Loading data into Rattle
- Assigning roles to the variables
- Transforming variables to solve data quality problems and to improve data format of our predictive model

In this chapter, we'll cover how we explore the data to understand it and find quality problems.

Datasets, observations, and variables

A **dataset** is a collection of data that we're going to use to create new predictions. There are different kinds of datasets. When we use a dataset for predictive analytics, we can consider a dataset like a table with columns and rows.

In a real-life problem, our dataset would be related to the problem we want to solve. If we want to predict which customer is most likely to buy a product, our dataset would probably contain customer and historic sales data. When we're learning, we need to find an appropriate dataset for our learning purposes. You can find a lot of example datasets on the Internet; in this chapter, and in the following one, we're going to use the Titanic passenger list as a dataset that has been taken from Kaggle.

Kaggle is the world's largest community of data scientists. On this website, you can even find data science competitions. We're not going to use the term **data science**, in this book, because there are a lot of new terms around analytics and we want to focus just on a few to avoid noise. Currently, we use this term to refer to an engineering area dedicated to collect, clean, and manipulate data to discover new knowledge. On www.kaggle.com, you can find different types of competitions; there are introductory competitions for beginners and competitions with monetary prices. You can access a competition, download the data and the problem description, and create your own solutions. An example of an introductory Kaggle competition is *Titanic: Machine Learning from Disaster*. You can download this dataset at https://www.kaggle.com/c/titanic-gettingStarted. We're going to use this dataset in this chapter and in *Chapter 3, Exploring and Understanding Your Data*.

A **dataset** is a matrix where each row is an observation or member of the dataset. In the Titanic passenger list, each observation contains the data related to a passenger. In a dataset, each column is a particular variable. In the passenger list, the column **Sex** is a variable. You can see a part of the Titanic passenger list in the following screenshot:

PassengerId	Survived	Pclass	Name	Sex	Age	SibSp	Parch	Ticket	Fare	Cabin	Embarked
1	0	3	Braund, Mr. Owen Harris	male	22	1	0	A/5 21171	7.25		S
2	1	1	Cumings, Mrs. John Bradley (Florence Briggs Thayer)	female	38	1	0	PC 17599	71.2833	C85	C
3	1	3	Heikkinen, Miss. Laina	female	26	0	0	STON/O2.	7.925		S
4	1	1	Futrelle, Mrs. Jacques Heath (Lily May Peel)	female	35	1	0	113803	53.1	C123	S
5	0	3	Allen, Mr. William Henry	male	35	0	0	373450	8.05		S
6	0	3	Moran, Mr. James	male		0	0	330877	8.4583		Q
7	0	1	McCarthy, Mr. Timothy J	male	54	0	0	17463	51.8625	E46	S
8	0	3	Palsson, Master. Gosta Leonard	male	2	3	1	349909	21.075		S
9	1	3	Johnson, Mrs. Oscar W (Elisabeth Vilhelmina Berg)	female	27	0	2	347742	11.1333		S
10	1	2	Nasser, Mrs. Nicholas (Adele Achem)	female	14	1	0	237736	30.0708		C
11	1	3	Sandstrom, Miss. Marguerite Rut	female	4	1	1	PP 9549	16.7	G6	S

Before we start, we need to understand our dataset. When we download a dataset from the Web, it usually has a variable description document.

The following is the variable description for our dataset:

- **Survived**: If the passenger survived, the value of this variable is set to 1, and if the passenger did not survive, it is set to 0.

- **Pclass**: This stands for the class the passenger was travelling by. This variable can have three possible values: 1, 2, and 3 (1 = first class; 2 = second class; 3 = third class).

- **Name**: This variable holds the name of the passenger.

- **Sex**: This variable has two possible values **male** or **female**.

- **Age**: This variable holds the age of the passenger.

- **SibSp**: This holds the number of siblings/spouses aboard.

- **Parch**: This holds the number of parents/children aboard.

- **Ticket**: This holds the ticket number.

- **Fare**: This variable holds the passenger's fare.

- **Cabin**: This variable holds the cabin number.

- **Embarked**: This is the port of embarkation. This variable has three possible values: **C**, **Q**, and **S** (**C** = Cherbourg; **Q** = Queenstown; **S** = Southampton).

For predictive purposes, there are two kinds of variables:

- **Output variables** or **target variables**: These are the variables we want to predict. In the passenger list, the variable **Survived** is an output variable. This means that we want to predict if a passenger will survive the sinking.

- **Input variables**: These are the variables we'll use to create a prediction. In the passenger list, the variable sex is an input variable.

Rattle refers to output variables as target variables. To avoid confusion, we're going to use the term target variable throughout this book. In this dataset, we've ten input variables (**Pclass**, **Name**, **Sex**, **Age**, **SibSp**, **Parch**, **Ticket**, **Fare**, **Cabin**, and **Embarked**) that we want to use to predict if this person is a potential customer or not. So in this example, our target variable is **Survived**.

In *Titanic: Machine Learning from Disaster*, the passenger list is divided into two CSV files: train.csv and test.csv. The file train.csv contains 891 observations or passengers; for each observation, we have a value for the variable **Survived**. It means that we know if the passenger survived or not. The second file, test.csv, contains only 418 customers, but in this file, we don't have the variable **Survived**. This means that we don't know if the passenger survived or not. The objective of the competition is to use the training file to create a model that predicts the value of the **Survived** variable in the test file. For this reason, the variable **Survived** is the target variable.

Rattle distinguishes two types of variables—numeric and categorical. A **numeric** variable describes a numerically measured value. In this dataset, **Age**, **SibSp**, **Parch**, and **Fare** are numeric variables.

A **categorical** variable is a variable that can be grouped into different categories. There are two types of categorical variables—ordinal and nominal. In an **ordinal categorical** variable the categories are represented by a number. In our dataset, **Pclass** is an ordinal categorical variable with three different categories or possible values 1, 2, and 3.

In a **nominal categorical** variable, the group is represented by a word label. In this dataset, **Sex** is an example of this type. This variable has only two possible values, and the values are the label, in this case, **male** and **female**.

Loading data

In Rattle, you have to explicitly declare the *role* of each variable. A variable can have five different roles:

- **Input**: The prediction process will use input variables to predict the value of the target variable.

- **Target**: The target variable is the output of our model.

- **Risk**: The risk variable is a measure of the target variable.

- **Ident** or **Identifier**: An identifier is a variable that identifies a unique occurrence of an object. In our preceding example, the variable **Person** is an identifier that identifies a unique person.

- **Ignore**: A variable marked Ignore will be ignored by the model. We'll come back to this role later-some variables can create noise and decrease the performance of your predictive model.

Rattle can load data from many data sources. Here are some options:

- Use the **Spreadsheet** option to load data from a **Comma Separated Value (CSV)** file.

- **Open Database Connectivity (ODBC)** is a standard to define database connectivity. Using this standard, you can load from most common databases. This will allow you to load data from ERP, CRM, data warehouse systems, and others.

- Use **Attribute-Relation File Format (ARFF)** to load data from Weka files. **Weka** is a machine learning software written in Java.

- You can also load R Datasets; these are tables loaded in memory using R. Currently, Rattle supports R data frames.

- The **RData file** option allows you to load an R Dataset that has been saved in a file, usually with the .Rdata extension.

- With the **Library** option, Rattle can load sample datasets provided by R packages.

- The **Corpus** option allows loading and processing a folder of documents.

- In the following screenshot, you can see a **Script** option, but this option is not implemented. It will be available in a future version.

In this book, we're going to load data from the CSV files to explain Rattle's functionalities. CSV is widely used to load data, and we'll find example datasets on the Internet as CSV files.

Loading a CSV File

As we've seen before, we'll use a CSV file from Kaggle to learn how to load a dataset into Rattle. Download the file train.csv from the competition page at http://www. kaggle.com/c/titanic-gettingStarted.

The steps to load the train.csv file are as follows:

1. Open Rattle and go to the **Data** tab:

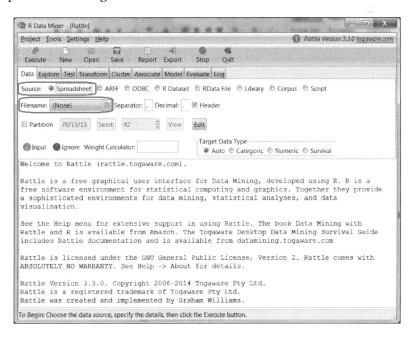

2. Select **Spreadsheet** as the data source and click on the **Filename** folder icon.

3. Select the file `train.csv` and click on **Open**:

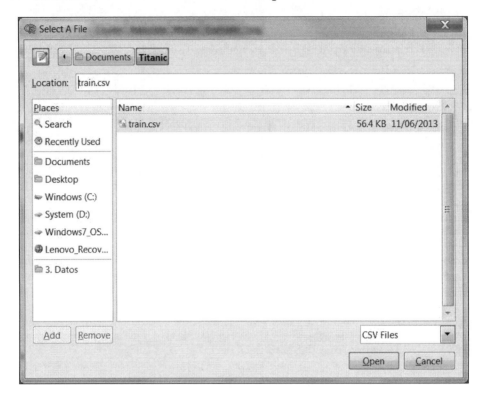

4. Finally, click the **Execute** button to load the dataset:

Rattle loads the data from the file, analyzes it, and guesses the structure of the dataset. Now we can start exploring the structure of our data. In the Rattle window, we can see that the loaded dataset has 891 observations with nine input variables and **Survived** as the target variable. We can change the role of each variable with the radio buttons. Note that **Age**, **Cabin**, and **Embarked** have missing values:

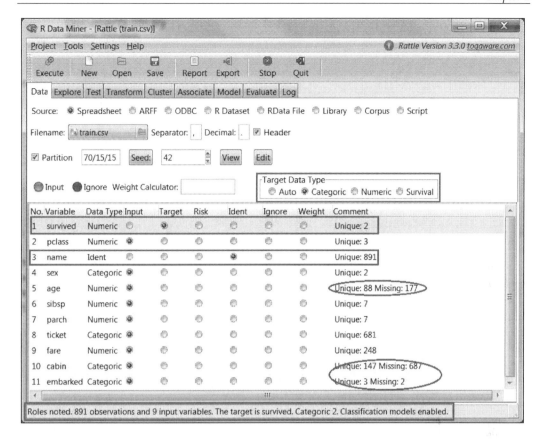

We'll focus on these missing values in the next section of this chapter.

The objective of this dataset is to predict whether or not a passenger will survive the sinking of the Titanic. Our target variable is **survived** and has two possible values:

- 0 (not survived)
- 1 (survived)

The variable **name** is an identifier that identifies a unique passenger. For this reason, it has 891 observations and 891 different values.

Make changes in the roles of the different variables and click on the **Execute** button to update the data. To save your work, click on the **Save** button and give it an appropriate file name.

The **Save** button will save our work, but it will not modify the data source (the CSV file).

In Rattle's **Data** tab, there are two useful buttons — **View** and **Edit**. With these buttons, you can edit and visualize your data. We also have a **Partition** check box, as you can see in the following screenshot:

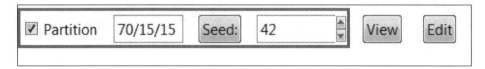

Generally, we split the datasets into three subsets of data — a training dataset, a validation dataset, and a testing dataset. We're going to leave this option for now and we'll come back to partitioning in *Chapter 5, Clustering and Other Unsupervised Learning Methods*, and *Chapter 6, Decision Trees and Other Supervised Learning Methods*.

The last option in data loading is **Weight Calculator**. This option allows us to enter a formula to give more importance to some observations.

 You can assign roles to variables automatically by modifying their names in the data source. When you load a variable with a name that starts with **ID**, Rattle marks it automatically as having a role of ident. You can also mark a variable as target, risk, and ignore using **Target**, **Risk**, and **Ignore**.

Transforming data

Data transformation and exploratory data analysis are two iterative steps. The objective is to improve the data quality to create a more accurate model. In order to transform your data, you need to understand it first. So, in real life, you can explore and transform iteratively until you are fine with your data.

For simplicity, we'll cover data transformation in this chapter and data exploration in the next chapter.

Data mining experts usually spend a lot of time preparing data before they start modeling. Preparing data is not as glamorous as creating predictive models but it has a great impact in the model performance. So, be patient and spend time to create a good dataset.

When we execute a transformation in a variable, Rattle doesn't modify the original variable. Rattle creates a new variable with a prefix that indicates the performed transformation and the name of the original variable. An example can be seen in the following screenshot:

No.	Variable	Data Type	Input	Target	Risk	Ident	Ignore	Weight	Comment
1	survived	Numeric	●	○	○	○	○	○	Unique: 2
2	pclass	Numeric	●	○	○	○	○	○	Unique: 3
3	name	Categoric	○	○	○	●	○	○	Unique: 891
4	sex	Categoric	●	○	○	○	○	○	Unique: 2
5	age	Numeric	●	○	○	○	○	○	Unique: 88 Missing: 177
6	sibsp	Numeric	●	○	○	○	○	○	Unique: 7
7	parch	Numeric	●	○	○	○	○	○	Unique: 7
8	ticket	Categoric	●	○	○	○	○	○	Unique: 681
9	fare	Numeric	○	○	○	○	●	○	Unique: 248
10	cabin	Categoric	●	○	○	○	○	○	Unique: 147 Missing: 687
11	embarked	Categoric	○	●	○	○	○	○	Unique: 3 Missing: 2
12	RRK_fare	Numeric	●	○	○	○	○	○	Unique: 248

We see the list of variables contained in Rattle after applying a rank transformation to the variable **fare**.

Transforming data with Rattle

Rattle's **Transform** tab offers four different types of transformations:

- **Rescale**
- **Impute**
- **Recode**
- **Cleanup**

These transformation options are shown in the following screenshot:

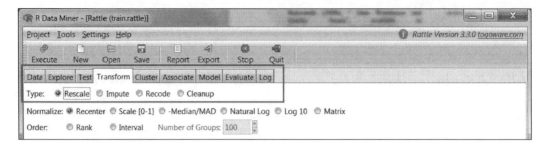

Rescaling data

In real life, measures use different scales; for example, in the Titanic passenger list, the minimum value for the variable **Age** is 0.42 and the maximum value is 80. For the variable **Fare**, the minimum is 0 and the maximum is 512.3. For this reason, a difference of 10 is a big difference for the variable **Age** and a small difference for **Fare**. Some algorithms and techniques need all variables with the same scale, and we need to adjust values measured on different scales to a common scale. **Rescaling** is the process of adjusting the numeric values of a variable to a different scale.

In Rattle, the **Rescale** option has two sub-options—**Normalize** and **Order**. To **Normalize** variables means to modify the values of the different observations to fit into a scale. The most common normalization is **Scale [0-1]**. If we apply this option to a variable, Rattle will map its values between 0 and 1. In the following table, we've used five values of the variable **Age** to create an example. As we've seen, the minimum value is 0 and the maximum 80. Rescaling the variable from 0 to 1, the minimum value is mapped to 0 and the maximum to 1. The intermediate values are mapped in between 0 and 1, as shown in the following table:

Age	New Value
0.42	0
5	0.057552149
19	0.233475748
54	0.673284745
80	1

Rattle provides two different **Order** transformations—**Rank** and **Interval**. With the **Rank** option, Rattle will convert variable values to a rank assigning 1 to the minimum value of the variable. We use this option when we're more interested in the relative position of value in the distribution than in the real value.

In our example, the first value of the variable age is 0.42 with the first position in our rank. The second position in the rank is for the value 0.67, and the third and fourth position in the rank has the same value, 0.75. In this case, Rattle doesn't use position three and four, it uses 3.5, as shown in the following table:

Age	Rank
0.42	1
0.67	2
0.75	3.5
0.75	3.5
0.83	5.5

Finally, **Interval** groups the values into different groups. Use the input box to choose the number of groups you want to create, as shown in the following screenshot:

Using **Interval** and the value **10** for **Number of Groups**, Rattle will create 10 groups and will label the groups **0, 1, 2, 3, 4, 5, 6, 7, 8,** and **9**. Depending on their value, Rattle will map each observation to a different group. The minimum value 0.4 will be in the group **0**; 80, the maximum value, will be mapped to group **9**.

Using the Impute option to deal with missing values

Sometimes, you will have incomplete observations with missing values for some variables. There are different reasons for missing values. Sometimes, data is manually collected, and not everybody collects it with the same accuracy. Sometimes data is collected from many sensors, and one of them could be temporarily out of order.

Detecting missing values could be difficult. In R, the value **NA**, which means Not Available, indicates a missing value, but there are a lot of data sources that codify a missing value with a concrete value. For numeric values, 0 or 99999 could identify a missing value. You'll need to explore your data carefully to find the real missing values. As we have seen, in the Titanic dataset, variables **Age**, **Cabin**, and **Embarked** have missing values.

With the **Impute** option, we can choose how we want to fill the missing values in our variables, as shown in this screenshot:

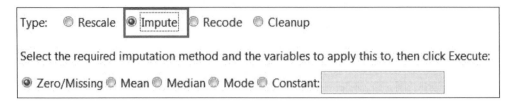

Rattle allows us to apply the following transformations to the missing values:

- **Zero/Missing**: Using this option, Rattle will replace all missing values in a numeric variable with 0 and missing values in a categorical variable with **Missing**.

- **Mean**: This option will use the mean to fill missing values in a numeric variable. Of course, we cannot use this option with a categorical variable.

- **Median**: With this option, we can replace missing values with the median. As with the **Mean** option, this option can only be used with numeric variables.

- **Mode**: Using the **Mode** option, Rattle will replace missing values with the most frequent value. This option can be used with both numeric as well as categorical variables.

- **Constant**: This option will allow us to enter a constant value to replace missing values. Like the **Mode** option, we can use it with both numeric as well as categorical variables.

Rattle has five different options, and if you need to use a different approach, you'll need to code in R, or fill the missing values before loading data into Rattle.

Now you probably must be thinking that the **Median**, **Mean**, and **Mode** options are very similar, and you don't know how to choose among the three different options. To choose one of these options, we need to see how values are distributed into the different observations. We'll see, in the next chapter, that the histogram is the best plot to see the value distribution in a variable, and you'll learn how to plot a histogram using Rattle.

To understand how to fill the missing values, you can analyze the histogram of the original variable, then apply a transformation and analyze the new histogram. With the example of the variable **Age**, we've created a histogram with the original variable (left-hand side). We've applied a **Zero** imputation and created a new histogram. When we apply a **Zero** imputation, we fill those values with all missing values. You will have something like the following graph:

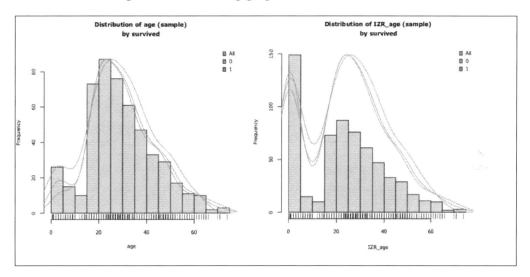

The histogram on the left shows the shape of the original variable **Age**; the mean is 29.7 years. In the Titanic dataset, the variable **Age** has 177 missing values. During the imputation, these 177 values are set to 0. This moves the mean of the distribution to 23.8. In this case, you can see a lot of people with 0 years. As we'll see, the performance of some techniques or algorithms can be affected by this change in the distribution shape.

Now, we can apply **Mean** imputation (fill the missing values with the mean), **Median** imputation (fill the missing values with the median), or **Mode** imputation (fill the missing values with mode).

These three screenshots show the distribution of the **Age** variable histogram after applying a **Mean** imputation (upper), a **Median** imputation (middle), and a **Mode** imputation (lower):

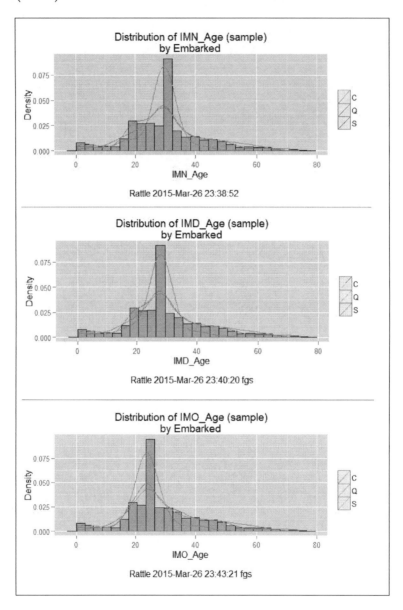

Additionally, you have to consider deleting all observations with missing values in the variable **Age**. This variable has 177 missing values in 891 observations; filling the gaps with a fixed value will probably produce a bad performance.

Recoding variables

We use the **Recode** option to transform the values of variables by distributing the values into different bins or by changing the type of the variable.

Binning

Some models and algorithms only work with categorical variables. **Binning** is an operation that can be useful to transform a numeric variable into a categorical variable. The original values that fall in a bin take the value that represents that bin.

This is how we bin a variable:

- Divide the range of values into a series of small intervals or bins
- Distribute each value into its interval or bin

To define the groups or bins, we have three options:

- Use **Quantiles** to create groups with the same number of observations
- Use **KMeans** to create groups of members based on the distance of the values
- Choose **Equal Width** to distribute the values of a variable into groups of the same width, as shown in this screenshot:

Like in this screenshot, try to apply an **Equal With** transformation (under **Binning**) to the variable **age**. Rattle will create **10** groups and will place each observation in a group.

To distribute values into different groups, you can also select **Type** as **Rescale**, and then **Order** as **Interval** and set **Number of Groups** as **10**, as shown in the following screenshot:

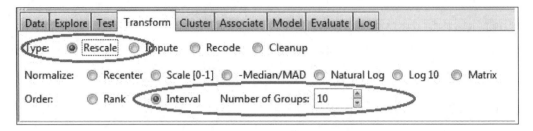

What is the difference between the two options? The variable **Age** is a numeric variable; when you use **Recode**, the result is a numeric variable. If you use **Binning**, the new variable is a categorical variable, as shown in this screenshot:

No.	Variable	Data Type and Number Missing
1	PassengerId	Numeric [1 to 891; unique=891; mean=446; median=446].
2	Survived	Numeric [0 to 1; unique=2; mean=0; median=0].
3	Pclass	Numeric [1 to 3; unique=3; mean=2; median=3].
4	Name	Categorical [891 levels].
5	Sex	Categorical [2 levels].
6	Age	Numeric [0.42 to 80.00; unique=88; mean=29.70; median=28.00; miss=177; ignored].
7	SibSp	Numeric [0 to 8; unique=7; mean=0; median=0].
8	Parch	Numeric [0 to 6; unique=7; mean=0; median=0].
9	Ticket	Categorical [681 levels].
10	Fare	Numeric [0.00 to 512.33; unique=248; mean=32.20; median=14.45].
11	Cabin	Categorical [147 levels; miss=687].
12	Embarked	Categorical [3 levels; miss=2].
13	RIN_Age_10	Numeric [0.00 to 9.00; unique=10; mean=3.29; median=3.00; miss=177].
14	BE10_Age	Categorical [10 levels; miss=177].

In the previous screenshot, we created **RIN_Age_10** using rescale and **BE10_Age** using binning.

Binning could also be used to reduce small observation errors. By replacing the original value by a representative value of the group, you will reduce the effect of small observation errors.

Indicator variables

As opposed to the previous section some algorithms (like many clustering models) only work with numeric variables. A simple technique to convert categorical variables into numeric variables is **indicator variables**. Take a categorical variable like **Level** with three categories—**Beginner**, **Medium**, and **Advanced**—and create three new variables called **Beginner indicator**, **Medium indicator**, and **Advanced indicator**. If the value of **Level** is Beginner, set variable **Beginner indicator** to **1** and the rest to **0**, as shown in this diagram:

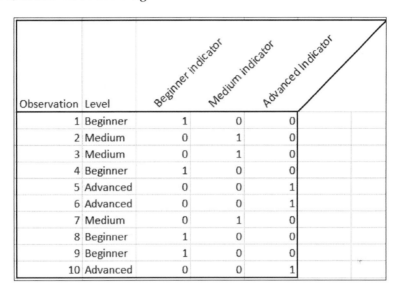

Observation	Level	Beginner indicator	Medium indicator	Advanced Indicator	
1	Beginner	1	0	0	
2	Medium	0	1	0	
3	Medium	0	1	0	
4	Beginner	1	0	0	
5	Advanced	0	0	1	
6	Advanced	0	0	1	
7	Medium	0	1	0	
8	Beginner	1	0	0	
9	Beginner	1	0	0	
10	Advanced	0	0	1	

In Rattle, the **Transform** tab has an **Indicator Variable** option. In order to apply this transformation, select the variable (in this case, **Level**), select **Indicator Variable**, and click on **Execute**, as shown in the following screenshot. Rattle will create a variable for each category belonging to the categorical variable:

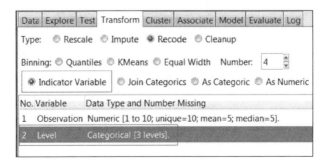

Join Categories

With the **Join Categories** option, Rattle will convert two categorical variables into a single one. In the following table, we've used Rattle to convert **Level** and **Sex** to a single variable:

Observation	Level	Sex	TJN_Level_Sex
1	Begginer	Male	Begginer_Male
2	Medium	Male	Medium_Male
3	Medium	Male	Medium_Male
4	Begginer	Male	Begginer_Male
5	Advanced	Female	Advanced_Female
6	Advanced	Female	Advanced_Female
7	Medium	Female	Medium_Female
8	Begginer	Female	Begginer_Female
9	Begginer	Female	Begginer_Female
10	Advanced	Male	Advanced_Male

As Category

Using the **As Category** option, you can convert numeric variables into categorical.

As Numeric

Using the **As Numeric** option, Rattle will convert categorical variable into numeric.

Cleaning up

The **Cleanup** option in the **Transform** tab allows you to delete columns and observations from your dataset, as shown in this screenshot:

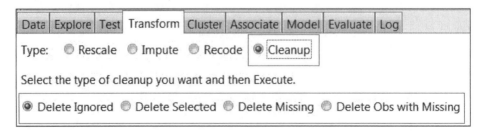

The following are the different available cleanup options:

- **Delete Ignored**: This will delete variables marked as ignore
- **Delete Selected**: This will delete the selected variables
- **Delete Missing**: This will delete all variables with any missing values
- **Delete Obs with Missing**: This will delete observations with missing values in the selected variable

You've learned how to transform variables. When Rattle transforms a variable, it doesn't modify the original one. It creates a new variable with the corresponding modification. If you apply a transformation to the variable **Age**, you will have the variable **Age** and the new one. Your algorithms only need one variable, the original or the transformed, so you have to change the role of the one not to be used to **Ignore**. By default, after the transformation, Rattle sets the original variable to **Ignore**. In the following screenshot, you can see the original variable **Age** set to **Ignore** and the new transformed variable set to **Input**:

No.	Variable	Data Type	Input	Target	Risk	Ident	Ignore	Weight	Comment
1	PassengerId	Numeric	○	○	○	◉	○	○	Unique: 891
2	Survived	Numeric	◉	○	○	○	○	○	Unique: 2
3	Pclass	Numeric	◉	○	○	○	○	○	Unique: 3
4	Name	Categoric	○	○	○	◉	○	○	Unique: 891
5	Sex	Categoric	◉	○	○	○	○	○	Unique: 2
6	Age	Numeric	○	○	○	○	◉	○	Unique: 88 Missing: 177
7	SibSp	Numeric	◉	○	○	○	○	○	Unique: 7
8	Parch	Numeric	◉	○	○	○	○	○	Unique: 7
9	Ticket	Categoric	◉	○	○	○	○	○	Unique: 681
10	Fare	Numeric	◉	○	○	○	○	○	Unique: 248
11	Cabin	Categoric	◉	○	○	○	○	○	Unique: 147 Missing: 687
12	Embarked	Categoric	○	◉	○	○	○	○	Unique: 3 Missing: 2
13	R01_Age	Numeric	◉	○	○	○	○	○	Unique: 88 Missing: 177

Exporting data

After data transformation, you have to export your new dataset, as shown in this screenshot:

In the main menu, press the **Export** icon; this will open a dialog window. Choose a directory and a filename and press **Save**. This book is the reference for Rattle.

Further learning

An extended explanation of data transformation in Rattle can be found in *Data Mining with Rattle and R*, by *Graham Williams, Springer*. Graham Williams is a well-known data scientist; he created and developed Rattle.

Summary

We started this chapter comparing the term *mise en place* used by professional chefs to the task of loading and preparing the data before we start creating predictive models.

During this chapter, we introduced the basic vocabulary to describe datasets, observations, and variables. We also saw how to load a CVS file into Rattle and described the most usual data transformations.

This chapter, as well as *Chapter 3, Exploring and Understanding Your Data,* covered the *mise en place* for our data. After going through these chapters, we'll be able to prepare our data to analyze it and discover hidden insights.

In the next chapter, we'll explore the dataset to have a better understanding and to find data quality problems. The next two chapters are tied because exploring the dataset and transforming it are complementary tasks.

When you are cooking, the quality of the ingredients has a great influence on the quality of your dish. Working with data is very similar; it's very hard to achieve good results if you use low quality data. For this reason, these two chapters are really important.

3
Exploring and Understanding Your Data

In the previous chapter, we've explained how to load data and how to transform it using Rattle. In this chapter, we're going to learn how use Rattle to:

- Summarize dataset characteristics
- Identify missing values in the data
- Create charts to represent data point distributions

We have two main objectives when we explore data. We would like to understand the problem we want to solve and we want to understand the structure of the dataset in order to choose the most appropriate predictive technique.

If you are a business analyst, Qlik Sense is a great tool to explore and understand your data. With Qlik Sense, you can find relationships between customers, products, and sales people in a very intuitive way. In the next chapter, we're going to learn how to use Qlik Sense to load and explore data.

As some predictive techniques are based on statistics, if you are preparing a dataset to apply a predictive technique, you would probably prefer a more formal or mathematical approach. We call this approach **Exploratory Data Analysis** (EDA). This is a large subject developed in 1997 by John W. Tuke

y. In this chapter, we'll see some EDA methods and concepts and we'll use Rattle to explore data. Mainly, we're going to use the **Test** tab to explore the data, but don't forget to start the exploration by looking at the data in tabular form.

Text summaries

The **Summary** option in the **Explore** tab provides us with some descriptive statistics such as **Summary**, **Describe**, **Basics**, **Kurtosis**, and **Skewness** reports. Descriptive statistics covers methods to summarize data. The **Summary** option also provides a very useful **Show Missing** report:

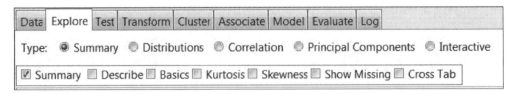

Summary reports

Rattle provides us with these summary reports:

- **Summary**
- **Describe**
- **Basics**
- **Kurtosis**
- **Skewness**

These reports summarize variable distributions and help to give an initial understanding of our data. In order to understand these reports, you only need a basic understanding of descriptive statistics.

Measures of central tendency – mean, median, and mode

For a variable, a measure of central tendency describes the center of the distribution as follows:

- **Mean**: The mean is the average and is the best central tendency measure if the distribution is normal.
- **Median**: Half of the observations have a lower value than this variable and the other half have a higher value. This is a good measure if there are extreme values.
- **Mode**: The mode is the most repeated value. In a histogram, the peak is the mode.

Measures of dispersion – range, quartiles, variance, and standard deviation

Measures of dispersion help us to summarize how spread out these scores are. To describe dispersion, Rattle provides us with some statistics, including the range, quartiles, absolute deviation, variance, and standard deviation. Dispersion gives us an idea of how the values for individual observations are spread out around the measure of central tendency.

Range

Range is the difference between the maximum and minimum values. The range can be useful to detect outliers if you are measuring variables with a critical low or high.

Quartiles

In a ranked variable, **quartiles** explain the spread of a dataset by breaking the dataset into quarters, which are described as follows:

- 25 percent of the observations have equal or lower value than the first quartile, or Q1

- 25 percent of the observations have equal or higher value than the third quartile, or Q3

- Half of the observations have a lower value than the median or the second quartile (Q2), and the other half have a higher value

Finally, we call the difference between Q3 and Q1 the **interquartile range**.

In the following screenshot, you can see the output of the **Summary** report for a numeric variable, **Age**, and for a categorical variable, **Embarked**:

```
        Age            Embarked
Min.    : 0.42      C    :117
1st Qu.:21.00       Q    : 56
Median :28.00       S    :449
Mean   :29.82       NA's:  1
3rd Qu.:39.00
Max.   :74.00
NA's   :123
```

For a numerical variable like **age**, this report tells us the minimum and maximum values (range), the quartiles, the mean, the median, and the number of missing values.

For a categorical variable like **embarked**, this report gives us the number of occurrences of each category and the number of missing values.

 You can find a more accurate description of quartile at this wiki: http://en.wikipedia.org/wiki/Quartile.

Variance

In a group of data, high **variance** means that the data points are widely spread; low variance means that the values are concentrated around the mean. Following is the formula for variance:

$$Variance = \frac{\sum (X - Median)^2}{N}$$

Here, **X** is the value of each observation and **N** is the total number of observations.

Standard deviation

The **standard deviation** is closely related to variance and it also measures the spread of values within a dataset. The formula is very simple – it is the square root of the variance. A low standard deviation indicates that the values are concentrated close to the mean; a high standard deviation indicates that the values are more spread out. The standard deviation is the most commonly used measure of spread because it is expressed in the same units as mean, whereas variance is expressed in square units.

Measures of the shape of the distribution – skewness and kurtosis

With **kurtosis** and **skewness**, we can have an intuition of the shape of the distribution of a variable. Kurtosis describes if a particular distribution is peaked and skewness measures the asymmetry of that distribution. A flatter distribution has a lower kurtosis.

In a negative skewed distribution, the left tail is longer than the right tail or the center of the data is moved to the right. For a positive skewed distribution, the longest tail is the right one or the center of the distribution is moved to the left.

As with quartiles, I suggest you take a look at the wiki for a more academic description:

- http://en.wikipedia.org/wiki/Kurtosis
- http://en.wikipedia.org/wiki/Skewness

In the following screenshot, you can see the **Basics** report for the variable **age**:

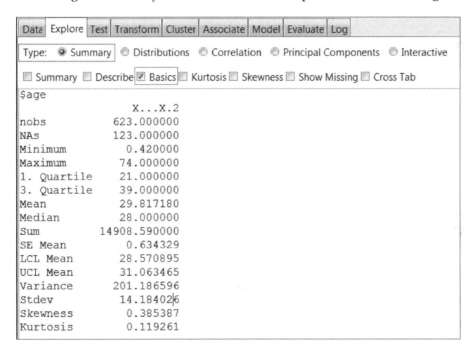

This report gives us the measures we've seen in this chapter, such as maximum, minimum, mean, median, standard deviation, variance, kurtosis, and skewness. There are still some strange measures we don't understand.

What are **SE Mean**, **LCL Mean**, and **UCL Mean**? They mean the following:

- **SE Mean**: This stands for the **Standard Error** of the mean
- **LCL Mean**: This stands for the **Lower Confidence Level** mean
- **UCL Mean**: This stands for the **Upper Confidence Level** mean

These measures explain the error margin of the mean and the confidence interval of the mean.

Showing missing values

Missing values is an important problem. For this reason, this report deserves special attention. We saw in the previous chapter how important missing values are and how we can fill these values; now we're going to see how to understand the impact of missing values in our dataset.

We're going to use the Titanic passenger list dataset. Perform the following steps:

1. Load the Titanic dataset into Rattle.
2. Go to the **Explore** tab.
3. Choose the **Summary** option.
4. Select the **Show Missing** values report.
5. Press the **Execute** button.

The preceding steps have been illustrated in the following screenshot:

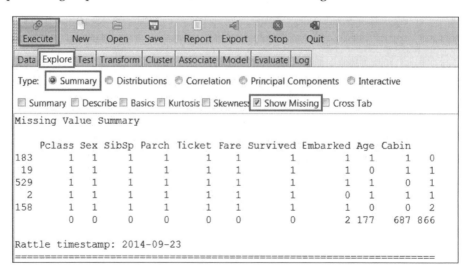

We've obtained a **Missing Value Summary** report as shown in the following screenshot. We're going to look at the report in more detail:

```
Missing Value Summary

    Pclass Sex SibSp Parch Ticket Fare Survived Embarked Age Cabin
183    1    1    1     1     1     1      1         1     1    1    0
 19    1    1    1     1     1     1      1         1     0    1    1
529    1    1    1     1  CENTRAL AREA    1         1     1    0    1
  2    1    1    1     1     1     1      1         0     1    1    1
158    1    1    1     1     1     1      1         1     0    0    2
       0    0    0     0     0     0      0         2   177  687  866

Rattle timestamp: 2014-09-23
========================================================================
```

As you can see in the highlighted part of the preceding screenshot, this report has a central area with a column for each variable. In this central area, each row corresponds to a pattern of observations, – **1** means that the value is present and **0** means the values is missing.

Now take a closer look at the first row. Below each variable, there is a **1**; this means that in this kind of observation, all variables have a value. What about the second row? The second row represents the observation that all variables have values except the variable **Age**.

On the left-hand side of the central area, there is a column. Each row in this column has a number representing the number of repetitions of the pattern. Looking at the first and second rows, there are **183** observations with no missing values and **19** observations with a missing value for the variable **Age**.

On the right-hand side of the central area, there is another column. Each row in this column has a number that tells how many missing variables there are in that pattern. Looking again at the first and second rows, they have **0** and **1** missing variables respectively.

Finally, under the central area, there is a row. In this row, each value is the number of total missing values that the variable has. In this example, **Embarked** has **2** missing values and **Age** has **177** missing values.

Remember that some datasets have dummy values for missing values. If you have a variable called price and you have observations with the value 0 for this variable, they are probably missing values. The Missing Value Summary report will not show these hidden missing values.

Visualizing distributions

In the last section, we discussed distributions and we saw some measures that describe them. In this section, we're going to see how to visualize distributions. Visualizations are more intuitive than numeric measures and they will help us to understand our data.

Rattle offers two different set of charts depending on the nature of the variables. For numeric variables, we can use **Box Plot**, **Histogram**, **Cumulative**, and **Benford**. And for categorical variables, Rattle provides us with **Bar Plot**, **Dot Plot**, and **Mosaic** charts. We're going to explore the most common visual representations.

Before using Rattle to plot charts, make sure that the **Advanced Graphics** option is unchecked. With this option checked, some charts like histograms will not be plotted. This is shown in the following screenshot:

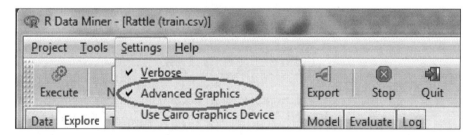

Numeric variables

We're going to use the variable **Age** of the Titanic passenger list to show the different types of charts with numeric variables. Load the data set, set the variable **Survived** as target, and go to the **Explore** tab and select the **Distributions** type. The central area of the screen is divided into two panels – the upper panel is reserved for the numeric variables and the lower one for categorical variables.

In the numeric variables area, you can see six variables (**Survived**, **Pclass**, **Age**, **SibSp**, **Parch**, and **Fare**) and four different plots (**Box Plot**, **Histogram**, **Cumulative**, and **Benford**). To plot a chart, you have to select the appropriate checkbox and click on the **Execute** button, as shown in the following screenshot:

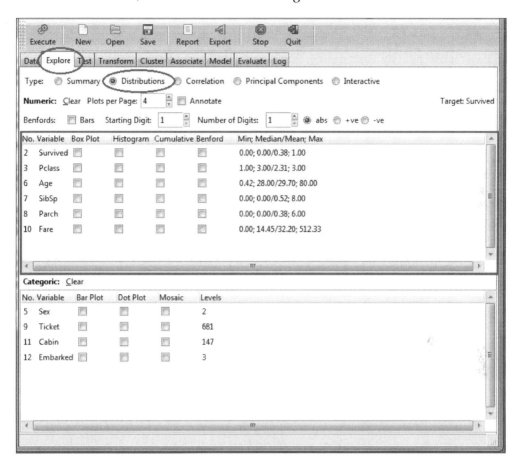

Box plots

The first chart we're going to discuss will be the **Box Plot**. We're going to plot a chart of the variable **Age** of the Titanic's passenger list. Select the **Annotate** checkbox in order to have the values of the data points labeled as shown in the following screenshot:

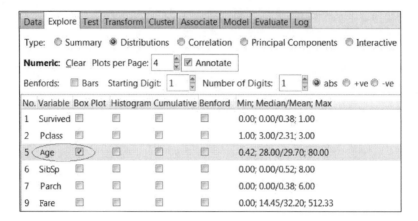

These plots summarize the distribution of a variable in a dataset. In the following screenshot, we can see the representation of the variable **Age**:

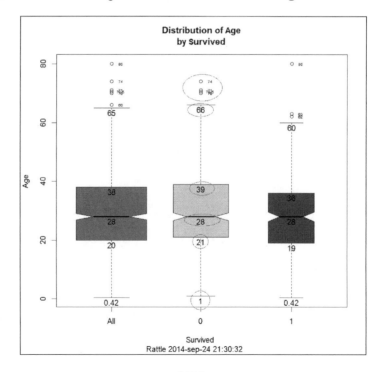

If you have identified the target variable when you loaded the dataset, Rattle will create a plot for all observations and a plot for every possible value of the target variable. In this example, the target variable **Survived** has two possible values, – 0 and 1.

We have highlighted some points of the central plot – the green part. In the center of the plot, the horizontal line labeled with a **28** is the median. The point labeled with a **21** is the first quartile, or Q1, and **39** represents the third quartile, or Q3. In this plot, the interquartile range is *39 - 21 = 18 (Q3 – Q1)*. The lower and upper points labeled with **1** and **66** are 1.5 times the interquartile range from the median. Points above the point labeled with a **66** are outliers.

Histograms

Histograms give us a quick view of the spread of a distribution. Rattle's histogram combines three charts in one, namely the R histogram (the bars), the density plot (the line), and the rug plot. The rug plot is marked with a red arrow in this screenshot:

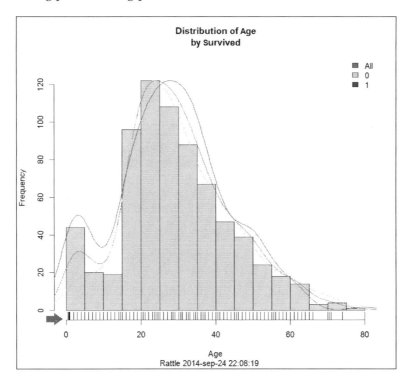

This histogram shows us the distribution in terms of age. The vertical bars are the original histogram. Every bar represents an **Age** range and the height of the bar represents the **Frequency** or the number of observations that fall in that age range. The density plot is a more accurate representation of the estimated values. Finally, in the rug plot, every line shows the exact value of an observation, as shown in the following screenshot:

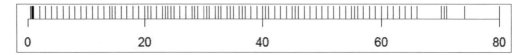

In the preceding histogram, we can see that most people on the Titanic were between **20** and **40** years of age.

Cumulative plots

The cumulative plot represents the percentage of the population that has a value than or equal to the value shown in the x axis. I've plotted the cumulative plot for the variable **Age**. If you look at the following screenshot, you can see that nearly 80 percent of the passengers were less than or equal to 40 years old.

We've circled the younger passengers. In this plot, like in the histogram we plotted before, we see that young people had a greater probability of survival.

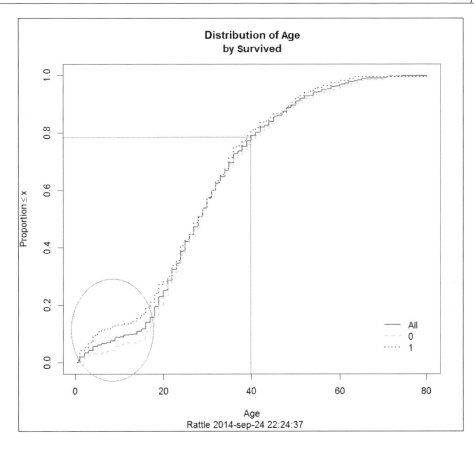

Categorical variables

We're now going to explore categorical variables. As with numeric variables, you have to load the Titanic dataset and set **Survived** as the target variable. Then go to the **Explore** tab and select the **Distributions** type.

To plot a new graph, you have to check the plot and the variable in the **Categoric** variable panel and click on **Execute**. This is illustrated in the following screenshot:

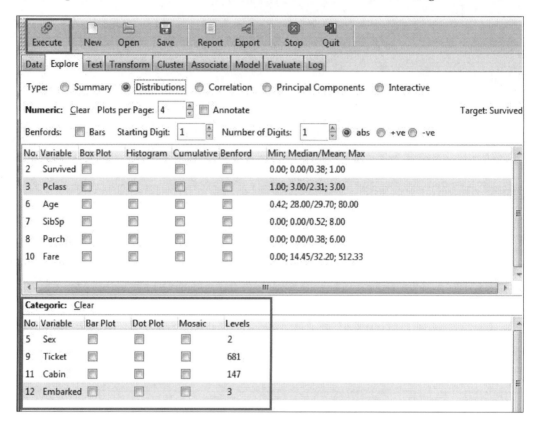

We'll use the variable **embarked** from the Titanic passenger list to plot a bar plot, a dot plot, and a mosaic plot.

Bar plots

The bar chart is probably the simplest and easiest to understand – it uses vertical or horizontal bars to compare among categories. In the following screenshot, we can see a bar chart of the variable **embarked**:

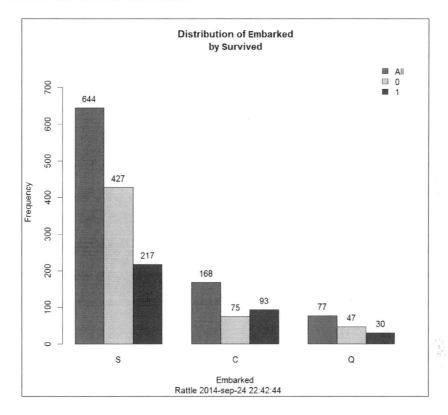

In the previous chapter, we introduced this dataset and we explained that the variable **embarked** has three possible values – **C** for Cherbourg, **Q** for Queenstown, and **S** for Southampton. If you look at this chart, it is quick and easy to see that most of the people (**644**) embarked in Southampton. Looking at the blue and green bars, we can see that around a third of the passengers that embarked at Southampton survived and around half of the passengers who embarked at Cherbourg survived.

Try to create a bar chart of the variable **sex** and you'll discover that 74.2 percent of females survived and only 18.9 percent of the males survived the Titanic disaster.

Mosaic plots

The mosaic plot shows the distribution of the values for a variable. Look at the following screenshot. At the top of the plot, there are three letters—**S, C,** and **Q**—representing the three harbors. Below each letter, there is a bar divided into two sub-bars (blue and green). We have highlighted the bar below **Q**, as shown in the following screenshot:

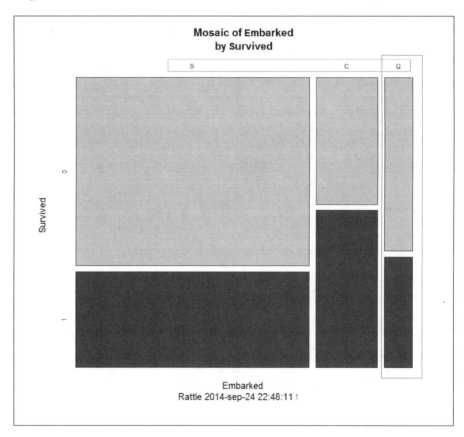

The width of this bar represents the number of occurrences. In our plot, the wider bar is the bar below **S**. This is the harbor where most of the people embarked. For each harbor, we have a green and a blue bar. The size of the green bar represents the number of people who didn't survive and the blue bar represents the number of people who survived.

As you can see, the mosaic plot gives us a fast understanding about how our data is distributed.

Correlations among input variables

An important step is to identify relationships among input variables. To measure this relationship, we use the correlation coefficient. **Correlation coefficient** is a number between +1 and -1. When two variables have a correlation coefficient close to +1, they have a strong positive correlation. A coefficient of exactly +1 indicates a perfect positive fit. A positive correlation between two variables means that both variables increase and decrease their values simultaneously. A correlation coefficient between two variables close to -1 shows that both variables have strong negative correlation. When two variables have a negative correlation, the value of one of the variables increases when the value of the other variable decreases. A correlation coefficient close to 0 or a weak correlation between two variables means that there is no linear relationship between those variables.

Coming back to the Titanic passenger list, I've selected the **Explore** tab, the **Correlation** sub-option, and I've clicked on the **Execute** button, as shown in this screenshot:

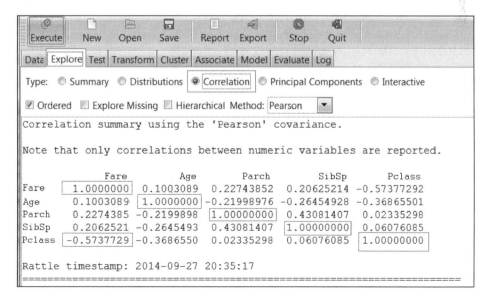

Of course, each variable has a correlation coefficient with itself of 1.0. Now look at the variable **Pclass** (passenger class). This variable has three possible values: 1 (first class), 2 (second class), and 3 (third class). This is a categorical variable because there are three possible groups or categories. These categories are ranked and we're going to use a numeric variable for that. In this way, Rattle can compute the correlation between **Pclass** and other numeric variables. Look at the correlation coefficient between **Fare** and **Pclass**; it is -0.573. Is there any relationship between **Fare** and **Pclass**? A correlation coefficient close to-0.6 indicates that there is some correlation between the two variables. What does this correlation between **Fare** and **Pclass** mean in real life, though? Usually, first class tickets are the most expensive, second class tickets are cheaper, and the third class tickets are the cheapest. Still, why is the relationship between **Pclass** and **Fare** negative? It is because a higher value of **Fare** (higher price) indicates a lower number of the variable **Pclass** (higher class).

The following chart is a visual representation of the correlation coefficients. By looking at the graph, you will see that the correlations coefficients are the same as in the previous report. Note that you need to enable the **Advanced Graphics** option inside the **Settings** menu for this:

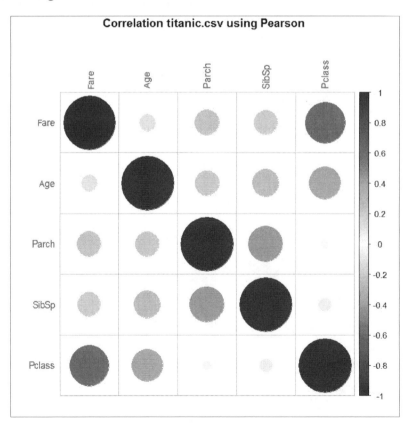

The Explore Missing and Hierarchical options

The **Explore Missing** option will help you to detect relationships between missing values in your dataset, as shown in the following screenshot:

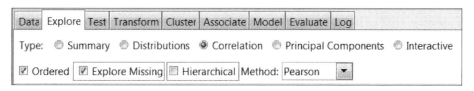

When two variables have a strong correlation in missing values, it means that when the value of a variable is not present, the second variable also tends to have a missing value.

The **Hierarchical** option uses a tree diagram graphical to represent the correlation between variables.

Further learning

In this chapter, we've introduced some EDA measures. If you want a more extensive EDA introduction, I recommend the *Exploratory Data Analysis* course on Coursera – www.coursera.org/course/exdata.

If you prefer going to the source, *Exploratory Data Analysis Paperback*, by John W. Tukey, is for you.

Wikipedia offers some useful insights into these EDA statistics concepts.

Summary

This chapter was divided into three main sections depending on how we are looking at data – tables, text summaries, and charts.

When we saw text summaries, we introduced Summary, Describe, Basics, Kurtosis, and Skewness reports. To understand these reports, we needed to remember some basic statistics concepts like mean, median, mode, range, quartile, interquartile range, variance, and standard deviation.

In this chapter, we also introduced some important charts – histograms, correlations, **Box Plot**, and **Bar Chart**.

In the next chapter, we'll learn how to load data into Qlik Sense and how to create data visualizations. We'll use some of the charts we introduced in this chapter. You'll see that Qlik Sense is more powerful for a business user who wants to understand his data and create a graphical representation of his data. Rattle and R are tools closer to statistics and some functionalities, like the correlations analysis, are very powerful; for this reason, we've introduced EDA using Rattle. After the next chapter, you'll be able to choose the tool that you feel more comfortable with for each task.

We'll continuing exploring data in the next chapter. After the next chapter, we'll start creating predictions with our data.

4
Creating Your First Qlik Sense Application

In the previous chapters, we've seen how to use Rattle to modify and explore our data. The exploration we've done is mainly a mathematical exploration. Qlik Sense is the perfect tool to explore and understand the data from a business point of view. Qlik Sense is easy and intuitive. In this chapter, we'll create a simple application in order to explore the basics of Qlik Sense.

To create a simple application, we'll follow these steps:

- Download an example dataset

- Learn how to load it into Qlik Sense

- Learn about the Qlik Sense data model and its application structure

- Learn how to create basic charts such as bar and pie charts

- To finish our application, we'll create some filters that will help us to select the desired information

- Finally, we'll learn to explore our dataset using Qlik Sense; at this point, we'll start answering basic business questions

Customer segmentation and customer buying behavior

Segmenting the customers means dividing our customers into groups relevant to our business. Customers are divided based on demography, behavior, and other indicators. Analyzing your customers and dividing them into different groups allows you to be more accurate in your marketing activities.

There are different types of customer segmentation; some of them are:

- Geographic segmentation
- Demographic segmentation
- Buying behavior segmentation
- Psychographic segmentation
- Segmentation by benefits
- Cultural segmentation

In this chapter, we'll develop an application that allows us to visually create customer segments based on different variables. In the next chapter, we'll create a system that will automatically segment our customers based on their shopping habits in the main product categories. The main objective of this application is improving our knowledge of our customers to address more effective marketing activities.

Loading data and creating a data model

In order to create an example application, I've downloaded a dataset from the Center for Machine Learning and Intelligent Systems at the University of California, Irvine. They have a dataset repository you can use for training purposes. The datasets are organized by task (clustering, classification, regression, and others), by attribute type, by domain area, and so on. This is a very useful resource to practice your new skills and we'll be using it again in this book.

 You can find more information from Bache, K. and Lichman, M. (2013); UCI Machine Learning Repository [http://archive.ics.uci.edu/ml]; Irvine, CA: University of California, School of Information and Computer Science.

In this chapter, we're going to use a dataset called **Wholesale customers Data Set**. The dataset is originated from a larger database – Abreu, N. (2011); Analise do perfil do cliente Recheio e desenvolvimento de um sistema promocional; Mestrado em Marketing, ISCTE-IUL, Lisbon. You can find the dataset on this page:

https://archive.ics.uci.edu/ml/datasets/Wholesale+customers#

The dataset contains 440 customers (observations) of a wholesale distributor. It includes the annual spending in monetary units on diverse product categories. The columns are explained as follows:

- **Fresh**: annual spending (per 1,000) on fresh products
- **Milk**: annual spending (per 1,000) on milk products
- **Grocery**: annual spending (per 1,000) on grocery products
- **Frozen**: annual spending (per 1,000) on frozen products
- **Detergents_Paper**: annual spending per 1,000) on detergents and paper
- **Delicatessen**: annual spending (per 1,000) on delicatessen products
- **Channel**: Horeca (value = **1**) or Retail (value = **2**)

 In the food industry, Horeca stands for Hotel, Restaurant, or Café, so a business that prepares and serves food.

- **Region**: Lisbon (value = **1**), Porto (value = **2**), or Other (value = **3**)

In the following screenshot, you can see what the data looks like:

Channel	Region	Fresh	Milk	Grocery	Frozen	Detergents_Paper	Delicassen
2	3	12669	9656	7561	214	2674	1338
2	3	7057	9810	9568	1762	3293	1776
2	3	6353	8808	7684	2405	3516	7844
1	3	13265	1196	4221	6404	507	1788
2	3	22615	5410	7198	3915	1777	5185
2	3	9413	8259	5126	666	1795	1451

An important difference between Rattle, or R, and Qlik Sense is that in Rattle, generally, our dataset is a simple table. Using Qlik Sense, we can easily work with more complex data models. Working with more complex data models allows us to discover hidden relationships. In this example, we have a table with customer data; if we're able to link the customer information with a salesperson or shipping information, our analysis would be richer.

In Qlik Sense Desktop, we have two ways to load data:

- We can use the **Data load editor** option
- We can use the **Quick data load** option

With the **Quick data load** option, you can load data by just dragging and dropping data files, but if you want to transform data into Qlik, you need to do it using the **Data load editor** option. We'll create our data model using only the **Quick data load** option, but we'll also see how we can do the same work using the **Data load editor** option.

Preparing the data

We're going to create a very simple data model.

Our data model has three tables. The main table, Customers, is the dataset we've downloaded. We also have two additional tables, Channel and Region. We're going to use the tables to convert from codes to descriptions; the value **1** in the field Region means Lisbon.

The original dataset contains six product categories – **Fresh**, **Frozen**, **Milk**, **Grocery**, **Delicatessen**, and **Detergents_Paper**. The six product categories can be grouped into two main categories – **Food** (**Fresh**, **Milk**, **Grocery**, **Frozen**, and **Delicatessen**) and **Detergents_Paper**. We'll create two new columns in the dataset called **Food** and **Total_Spent**. The new variable **Food** will contain the sum of **Fresh**, **Milk**, **Grocery**, **Frozen**, and **Delicatessen**. The new variable **Total_Spent** will contain the total annual expenditure for each customer. We can create the new fields in two ways. We can use a spreadsheet tool to create these new columns and set it as a CSV file to save the resulting data. We can also use the **Data load editor** to do it. In this example, we'll use the **Data load editor** to create these two variables and a third variable called **Customer_ID**. The variable **Customer_ID** will be a unique identifier for each customer.

In the original dataset, we need six values to represent the annual expenditure of a customer. It's hard to represent six variables in a two-dimensional chart. In the modified dataset, we can use two values—**Food** and **Detergents_Paper**—to summarize the six original values. In this way, we can graphically represent the annual expenditure of a customer by a point in a plane. This is a trick to see your customers in an easy way.

You can see our data model in the following diagram:

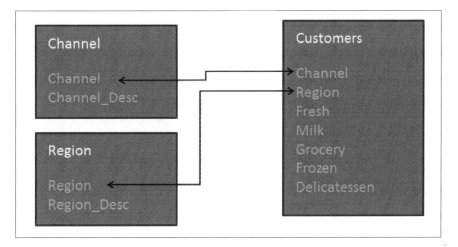

In the preceding diagram, we can see that the three tables are associated. To associate two tables, Qlik Sense only needs to find two fields with the same name. If Qlik Sense finds a field called Channel in the Customers table and a field with the same name in the Channel table, its associative engine assumes that the two fields mean the same and associates the tables.

Create two CSV or Excel files containing the following two smaller tables. These tables will have the common columns Channel and Region when compared with the main Customers table:

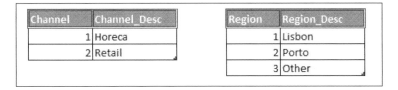

Open Qlik Sense Desktop and in the pop-up window, select **Create new app**, name it, and open the new application.

A Qlik Sense application has a main menu. We'll use this menu to move between the **App overview**, **Data load editor**, **Data model viewer**, and **Open hub** options, as shown here:

Drag the customers file you have modified and drop it over your new application. A window showing the data you are going to load will appear; simply click on the **Load data** button. After these instructions are followed, you will see a screen similar to this:

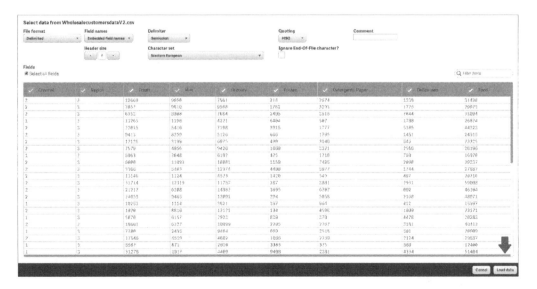

A pop-up window will inform you that the data has been loaded. Close the window and load the **Channel** and **Region** files (the two smaller CSV files that we created earlier). Every time you try to add a new data file, Qlik Sense will ask you if you want to replace or add data; choose **Add data** as shown in the following screenshot:

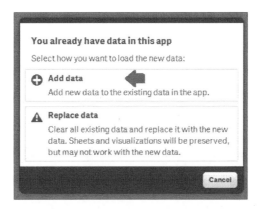

Now we can review our work. Open the **Data model viewer** option. Qlik Sense opens the data model we've just built.

Check the data model we've just created. Close to the fields `Channel` and `Region`, there is an icon representing a key. I've circled the icon to make it easier to identify. This icon means that Qlik uses this field to associate a table with another one, as shown in the following screenshot:

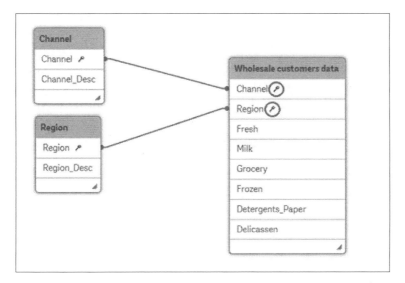

To load this data we've used the Quick data load functionality. This functionality is only present in Qlik Sense Desktop, and is not present in the server version of the product. Qlik Sense, as a platform not as a personal tool, focus on data governance. For an analytic tool data governance are mechanisms to ensure the data loaded in the system meets the organization's standards. For this reason this functionality is not present in in Qlik Sense.

Qlik Sense Desktop Quick data load functionality has done a lot of work for us. In order to understand what happened, we'll review the Data load editor and we'll use it to create the three new variables.

Look at the left-hand side vertical bar; Qlik Sense has created a sheet for every file that we've loaded. Look at this sheet and you will find a LOAD sentence like the one shown in the following screenshot:

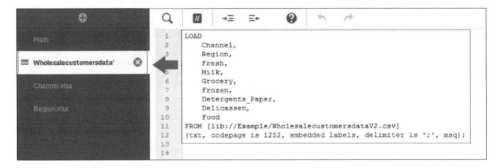

This LOAD sentence is very useful; if you want, you can modify data here before loading it. As we've said before, we want to add three new columns to this table – **Customer_ID**, **Food**, and **Total_Spent**. We can do this simply by adding the columns to the spreadsheet or by using the Qlik **Data load editor** option. In this example, we're going to use the **Data load editor** option.

Change the code as shown in the following screenshot and click on the **Load data** button. Qlik Sense will reload all data files. With this code, you've calculated the new field in Qlik Sense instead of doing it in the CSV file or the Excel spreadsheet:

The first line adds a number and labels it as `Customer_ID`. The function `RowNo()` returns the number of the row. In this dataset, each row is a different customer, so with this line of code, we'll add an identifier to each customer. The last two lines add the new variables **Food** and **Total_Spent**.

Open the **Data model viewer** option again; now you can see the three fields that we've just created. This is shown in the following screenshot:

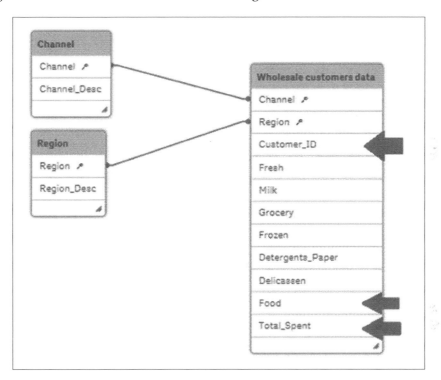

As you've seen, you can create the same data model using your favorite spreadsheet tool and load it to Qlik Sense or use the **Data load editor** option. The **Data load editor** option is a powerful Qlik Sense feature. Like in other self-service visualization tools, Qlik Sense has the option to load data without writing a line of code, but you also have a powerful data loading and transformation tool. Personally, I prefer the **Data load editor** option because it provides me with precise control over my data.

Creating a simple data app

As we've seen in *Chapter 1, Getting Ready with Predictive Analytics*, a Qlik Sense application is based on different sheets. In this section, we'll learn how to add a new sheet in your application and how to add basic charts and filters.

In the Qlik Sense main menu, choose **App overview** to open your application. A new Qlik Sense application always has an empty sheet called **My new sheet**, and you always have the option of adding a new one. This option is shown in the following screenshot:

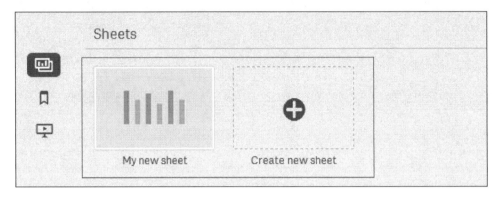

Now you are on an empty sheet. In order to modify a Qlik Sense sheet, you need to turn the **Edit** mode on. You can do this by clicking on the **Edit** mode to add new visual components, as shown in this screenshot:

Associative logic

Before learning how to create charts, we'll learn how associative logic works. **Associative logic** is a key functionality in Qlik Sense – it allows a business user without technical knowledge to explore the data.

In the following screenshot, we'll see the Qlik Sense main screen in **the Edit** mode. The screen is divided into three areas. In the center pane, you can see the sheet you're developing; the current screenshot shows an empty sheet. The right-hand pane shows the properties of the active object. In this case, the right-hand pane shows the sheet properties – **Title**, **Description**, and **Thumbnail**. The left-hand pane has a tab row with three options – **Charts**, **Fields**, and **Master items**; in this chapter, we'll use **Charts** and **Fields**, as shown here:

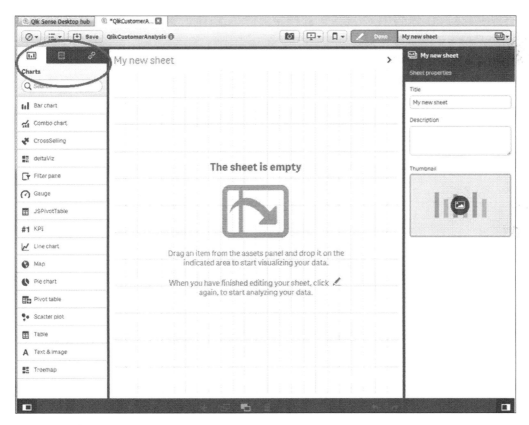

From the left-hand side tab row, select **Fields**; you'll see all fields in alphabetical order. Drag the **Channel_Desc** field and drop it into the central area, as shown in the following screenshot:

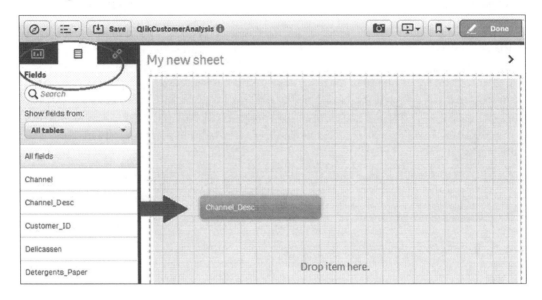

This action will add a filter pane to your new sheet. The filter pane has four arrows – up, down, right, and left. Use these arrows to move and resize the filter pane. You will be able to move and resize all visual objects in Qlik Sense, as shown here:

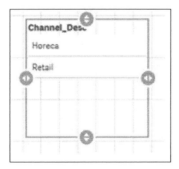

After placing **Channel_Desc**, add two fields as pane filters in your sheet – **Region_Desc** and **Customer_ID**. Finally, click on the **Done** button to exit the edit mode, as shown in the following screenshot:

You've learned in *Chapter 1, Getting Ready with Predictive Analysis,* how to use a filter in Qlik Sense. The following screenshot illustrates that the two filters that have been selected, turned green in color. Use these two filters to answer the question: which retail customers do I have in Porto?

You've selected **Retail** and **Porto** in the **Channel_Desc** and **Region_Desc** filters. In the **Customer_ID** pane, you can see some customers with a white background and some customers with a dark grey background. The customers with the white background are customers associated to **Retail** and **Porto**, so these customers are **Retail** customers from **Porto**. The dark grey customers are not related to **Porto** and **Retail**, so they are not **Retail** customers from **Porto**.

Using filters, a business user with no technical knowledge can ask everything about his dataset.

Creating charts

Before starting to create **chart** diagrams, delete the filters we've created in the previous section or create a new sheet.

To create a Qlik Sense visualization, you need to know three important things:

- The type of **chart** you are going to use
- The **dimension** objects you are going to use in your analysis
- The metric or metrics

We're going to start with a very basic **chart**. Our objective is to create a **pie chart** like the chart in the following screenshot. This chart explains the distribution of our customers between two channels – **Horeca** and **Retail**:

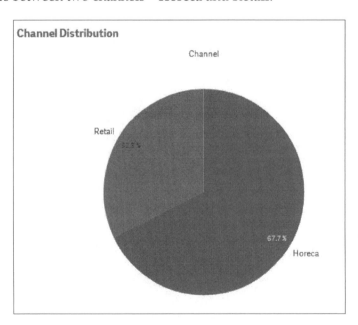

In this pie chart, the dimension is **Channel** and the measure is the number of customers. On the left-hand side of the following screenshot, there is a bar with all of the different charts that Qlik Sense provides. Drag a pie chart and drop it into the central area as shown in the following screenshot. Change the size of the chart with the orange lines and place it wherever you prefer:

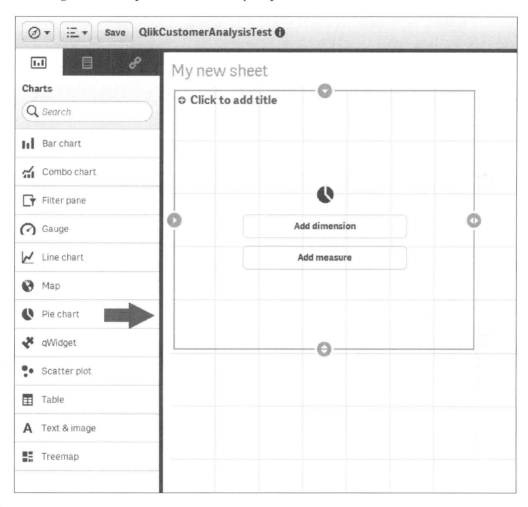

In order to finish the pie chart, you need to choose a **dimension** and a **measure**, and change the **title** to an appropriate one. In order to add **Channel** as the dimension, click on **Add measure** and select **Channel_Desc**. Finally, add **Count([Customer_ID])** as the measure. This is shown in the following screenshot:

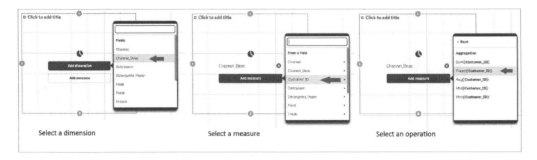

Close the edit mode by clicking on **Done**:

You've finished your first pie chart and it tells you that 67.7 percent of your customers belong to **Horeca** and only 32.3 percent belong to **Retail**.

Now I would like to understand which customers spend more money. I will create a bar chart using **Channel_Desc** as the dimension and the average money spent as the measure. Drag-and-drop a bar chart into the central area, change its **title**, and select **Channel_Desc** as the dimension and **avg([Total_Spent])** as the measure. Your bar chart might look similar to the following screenshot:

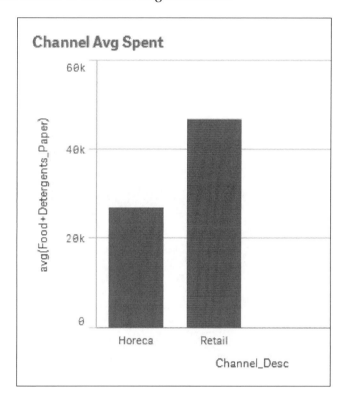

You've created a chart that tells you that, on average, **Retail** customers spend more money than **Horeca** customers. I would like to improve this bar chart. Turn the **Edit** mode on and click on **Bar chart** to select it. On the right-hand side, you have a bar with the chart properties. For a bar chart, the properties are organized around five areas:

- **Dimensions**
- **Measures**
- **Sorting**
- **Add-ons**
- **Appearance**

These areas are shown in the following screenshot:

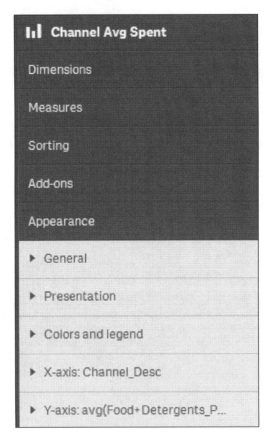

Bar charts are a very good measure to see the difference in the average money spent by **Horeca** and **Retail** customers, but it's hard to see the exact value. For this reason, we'll put the exact value in the chart. We're going to change the labels for the dimension and the measure, from **Channel_Desc** and **Avg(Total_Spent)** to `Channel` and `Avg. Spent`, by following these steps:

1. Expand the **Dimensions** menu and write a new label in the **Label** text field.

2. Expand the **Measures** menu and write an appropriate name in the **Label** text field.

3. Expand the **Appearance** menu and turn the **Value labels** option on to see the exact value on the chart.

These steps are demonstrated in the following screenshot:

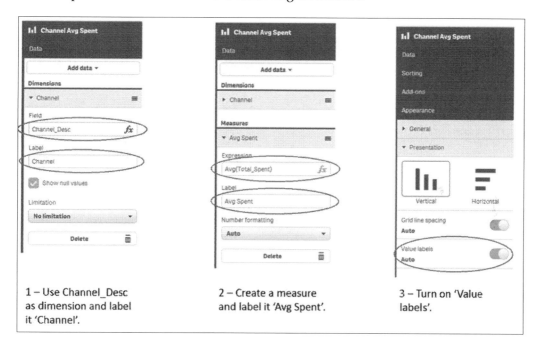

1 – Use Channel_Desc as dimension and label it 'Channel'.

2 – Create a measure and label it 'Avg Spent'.

3 – Turn on 'Value labels'.

Finally, in the pie chart we created before this bar chart, **Retail** and **Horeca** customers appeared colored in blue and red, but in the bar chart, all bars are blue. In order to have a consistent application in terms of color, we'll change the color properties of the bar chart to have the same colors as in the pie chart. As you can see in the following screenshot, we need to turn off the **Auto** mode from the **Color** option and set it to **By dimension**:

Now we've created two plots that explain that we have more **Horeca** customers than **Retail** customers, but on average our **Retail** customers spend more money on our business:

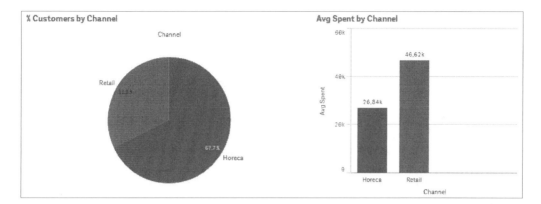

I know that, on average, I'm earning more money with the **Retail** channel customers, but my next question is: in which channel am I earning more money in absolute terms?

Create a new bar chart with **Channel_Desc** as the dimension and the following six measures:

- **Sum([Delicassen])** – label it `Delicatessen`
- **Sum([Detergents_Paper])** – label it `Detergents`
- **Sum([Fresh])** – label it `Fresh`
- **Sum([Frozen])** – label it `Frozen`
- **Sum([Grocery])** – label it `Grocery`
- **Sum([Milk])** – label it `Milk`

In the **Appearance** menu, expand the **Presentation** submenu. In this bar chart, we'll see six different measures; we can see these measures grouped in six different bars for **Retail** and six for **Horeca**. We also can see the six metrics stacked in one single bar. In this case, stacking the metrics in a single bar has the advantage of us being easily able to see the total money spent. This is illustrated in the following screenshot:

With this new bar chart, you can see that we're earning 8 million with our **Horeca** customers and 6.62 million with our **Retail** customers. We can also see that **Horeca** customers spend 4 million in **Fresh** products. The **Retail** customers spend 2.32 million in **Grocery**

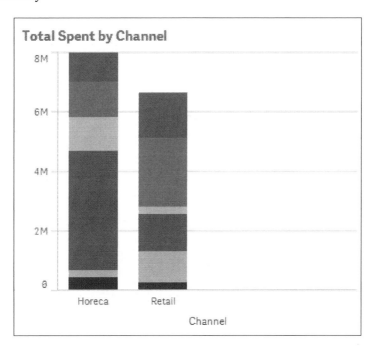

We've created a pie chart and two bar charts to understand how **Horeca** and **Retail** customers are buying our products. Now, repeat the three charts by changing the dimension from Channel_Desc to Region_Desc, as shown in the following screenshot:

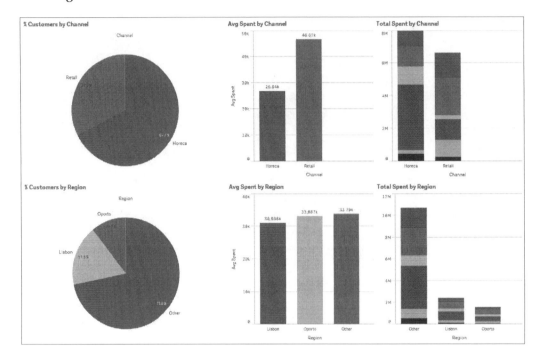

To finish our application, we're going to create a table with our top customers and two filters. Tables are different from regular charts because tables have columns; when you add a new column to a table, Qlik Sense asks you if the new column is a dimension or a measure. To create a table of top customers, drag a table and drop it into the central area. Choose **Customer_ID** as the dimension and **sum(Total_Spent)** as the measure. Limit the number of customers to **10** and sort by **Total Spent**, as shown here:

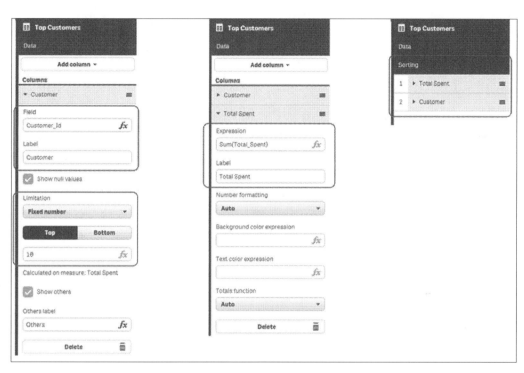

To finish the application, we'll add two filters. Go to the left-hand side bar, open the **Fields** list, and drag-and-drop **Channel_Desc** and **Region_Desc** into the central area:

Click on the **Save** button on the top bar and turn the **Edit** mode off. We've finished our first application. In the next section, we'll use this application to answer business questions:

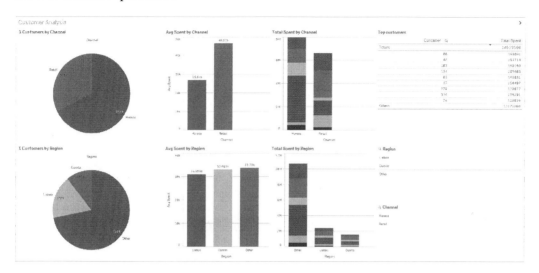

These charts tell us that 67.7 percent of our customers were **Horeca** customers and only 32.3 percent were **Retail** customers. On average, **Retail** customers spent more money on our products, but in absolute values, **Horeca** customers spent more money.

We have three regions – **Lisbon**, **Porto**, and **Others**. 17.5 percent of our customers were located in **Lisbon**, 10.7 percent in **Porto**, and 71.8 percent in **Other** regions. The average money spent is similar in all the regions, but the total spent is higher in **Other** regions than in **Lisbon** and **Porto**.

Now, we're going to use the filters to respond to more questions.

Analyzing your data

Our new application has two filters we can use to get a response to our questions. Select **Horeca** in the **Channel** filters. The application responds by actualizing the data. Now everything you see is related to the **Horeca** customers. Use the green or red buttons to confirm or cancel your selection. This is depicted in the following screenshot:

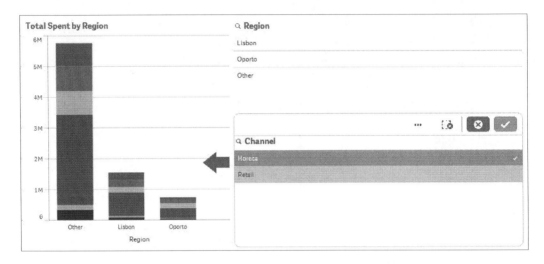

In the following screenshot, I've selected **Horeca** and **Porto**, and in the **Top Customers** table, I can see the top 10 **Horeca** customers in **Porto**. Now you can use the filters and the visualizations we've created to answer your own questions:

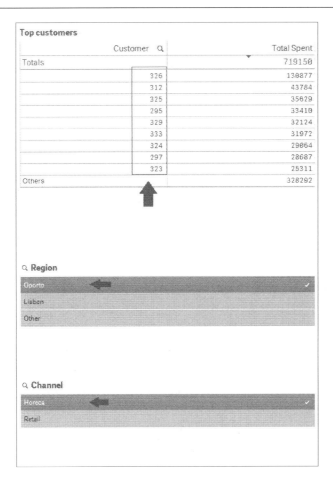

You can filter the data using the filters we've put in the application or you can filter the data by clicking on the charts.

Finally, I've created a new sheet called **360° Analysis**. In this last sheet, we analyze the customer average money spent and the total money spent in the two different sales channels, the three regions, and the six different product categories. The following screenshot represents all this:

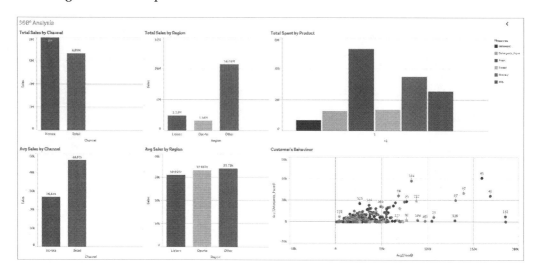

In the bottom-right, you can see a scatter plot. In this chart, each point represents a customer. The *y* axis represents the money spent on **Detergents_Paper** and the *x* axis represents the money spent on **Food**. At the beginning of this chapter, we created the field **Food** to be able to represent the customer's behavior on a plane.

Now try to select the **Retail** customers directly on a chart. All of the charts will update automatically to represent only **Retail** customers.

Finally, cancel your selection and select a single customer. On the **Total Spent by Product** bar chart, you can see the money spent by this customer in each category.

Now it's your turn to try to create new charts with Qlik Sense and explore your customers' characteristics even more.

Further learning

In this chapter, we've learned three main things about Qlik Sense – how to load and transform data, how to make selections to filter data, and how to create basic visualizations.

To find out more information about these features, I suggest you go through this document created by Michael Tarallo on the Qlik Community – `https://community.qlik.com/docs/DOC-6932`.

For data loading, you will find a section in the previous document called *Data Loading & Modeling*, but we especially like *Power of Qlik Script*, a series of three videos. There is a special video to learn how associative logic works, called *Working with Selections*, and in the *Apps & Visualizations* sections, you'll find videos that explain how to create data visualizations.

Qlik Community is a very active users' community around the Qlik platform. You will find a lot of resources related to Qlik Sense on this site. I strongly recommend you to register with *Qlik Community*.

Summary

In this chapter, we saw how to use Qlik Sense to create an application that helps us to analyze our customer data. We used a simple dataset with just 440 customers that we downloaded from the University of California website mentioned earlier. The dataset contained only two dimensions—channel and region—and six measures—**Fresh**, **Frozen**, **Milk**, **Grocery**, **Delicatessen**, and **Detergents_Paper**.

We learned how to load a dataset from a CSV file. We created a data model and uploaded additional tables created in a spreadsheet editor. Finally, we saw that we can create additional fields in a table using the spreadsheet editor or the data load editor. We also saw that the data load editor provides a lot of control over the data.

After creating the data model, we learned what associative logic is and how a business user can slice and dice his data using it.

Finally, we learned how to create basic visualizations using Qlik Sense, and we created our first Qlik Sense app.

In the next chapter, we'll use Rattle to segment the customers automatically based on their annual money spent in the different product categories. This segmentation will show us the data in a different light.

In *Chapter 8*, *Visualizations, Data Applications, Dashboards, and Data Storytelling*, we'll improve our knowledge of Qlik Sense and learn to create useful and attractive visualizations.

5
Clustering and Other Unsupervised Learning Methods

In this chapter, we will:

- Define machine learning
- Introduce unsupervised and supervised methods
- Focus on **K-means**, a classic machine learning algorithm, in detail

We'll use K-means to improve the application we created in *Chapter 4, Creating Your First Qlik Sense Application*. In *Chapter 4, Creating Your First Qlik Sense Application*, we created a Qlik Sense application to understand our customers' behavior. In this chapter, we'll create clusters of customers based on their annual money spent. This will give us a new insight. Being able to group our customers based on their annual money spent will allow us to see the profitability of each customer group and deliver more profitable marketing campaigns or create tailored discounts.

Finally, we'll see hierarchical clustering, different clustering methods, and association rules. Association rules are generally used for market basket analysis.

Machine learning – unsupervised and supervised learning

Machine Learning (ML) is a set of techniques and algorithms that gives computers the ability to learn. These techniques are generic and can be used in various fields. Data mining uses ML techniques to create insights and predictions from data.

In data mining, we usually divide ML methods into two main groups – supervised learning and unsupervised learning. A computer can learn with the help of a teacher (supervised learning) or can discover new knowledge without the assistance of a teacher (unsupervised learning).

In **supervised learning**, the learner is trained with a set of examples (dataset) that contains the right answer; we call it the **training dataset**. We call the dataset that contains the answers a **labeled dataset**, because each observation is labeled with its answer. In supervised learning, you are supervising the computer, giving it the right answers. For example, a bank can try to predict the borrower's chance of defaulting on credit loans based on the experience of past credit loans. The training dataset would contain data from past credit loans, including if the borrower was a defaulter or not.

In **unsupervised learning**, our dataset doesn't have the right answers and the learner tries to discover hidden patterns in the data. In this way, we call it unsupervised learning because we're not supervising the computer by giving it the right answers. A classic example is trying to create a classification of customers. The model tries to discover similarities between customers.

In some machine learning problems, we don't have a dataset that contains past observations. These datasets are not labeled with the correct answers and we call them **unlabeled datasets**.

In traditional data mining, the terms **descriptive analytics** and **predictive analytics** are used for unsupervised learning and supervised learning.

In unsupervised learning, there is no target variable. The objective of unsupervised learning or descriptive analytics is to discover the hidden structure of data. There are two main unsupervised learning techniques offered by Rattle:

- Cluster analysis
- Association analysis

Cluster analysis

Sometimes, we have a group of observations and we need to split it into a number of subsets of similar observations. **Cluster analysis** is a group of techniques that will help you to discover these similarities between observations.

Market segmentation is an example of cluster analysis. You can use cluster analysis when you have a lot of customers and you want to divide them into different market segments, but you don't know how to create these segments.

Remember the application we developed in *Chapter 4, Creating Your First Qlik Sense Application*? We started with a dataset containing 440 customers; each observation contained the money the amount of customer spent in six different product categories. We used Qlik Sense to create an application that helps us to understand our customers. Sometimes, especially with a large amount of customers, we need some help to understand our data. Clustering can help us to create different customer groups based on their buying behavior.

In Rattle's **Cluster** tab, there are four cluster algorithms:

- **KMeans**
- **EwKm**
- **Hierarchical**
- **BiCluster**

The two most popular families of cluster algorithms are hierarchical clustering and centroid-based clustering:

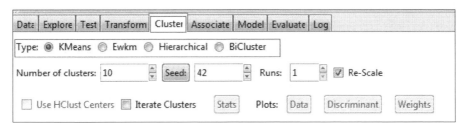

Centroid-based clustering the using K-means algorithm

I'm going to use K-means as an example of this family because it is the most popular.

With this algorithm, a cluster is represented by a point or center called the **centroid**. In the initialization step of K-means, we need to create *k* number of centroids; usually, the centroids are initialized randomly. In the following diagram, the observations or objects are represented with a point and three centroids are represented with three colored stars:

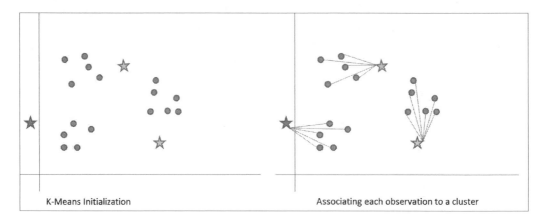

K-Means Initialization   Associating each observation to a cluster

After this initialization step, the algorithm enters into an iteration with two operations. The computer associates each object with the nearest centroid, creating *k* clusters. Now, the computer has to recalculate the centroids' position. The new position is the mean of each attribute of every cluster member.

This example is very simple, but in real life, when the algorithm associates the observations with the new centroids, some observations move from one cluster to the other.

The algorithm iterates by recalculating centroids and assigning observations to each cluster until some finalization condition is reached, as shown in this diagram:

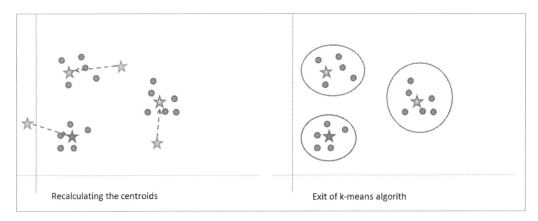

Recalculating the centroids   Exit of k-means algorith

The inputs of a K-means algorithm are the observations and the number of clusters, k. The final result of a K-means algorithm are k centroids that represent each cluster and the observations associated with each cluster.

The drawbacks of this technique are:

- You need to know or decide the number of clusters, k.
- The result of the algorithm has a big dependence on k.
- The result of the algorithm depends on where the centroids are initialized.
- There is no guarantee that the result is the optimum result. The algorithm can iterate around a local optimum.

In order to avoid a local optimum, you can run the algorithm many times, starting with different centroids' positions. To compare the different runs, you can use the cluster's distortion – the sum of the squared distances between each observation and its centroids.

Customer segmentation with K-means clustering

We're going to use the wholesale customer dataset we downloaded from the Center for Machine Learning and Intelligent Systems at the University of California, Irvine, in *Chapter 4, Creating Your First Qlik Sense Application*. You can download the dataset from here – `https://archive.ics.uci.edu/ml/datasets/Wholesale+customers#`.

As we saw in *Chapter 4, Creating Your First Qlik Sense Application*, the dataset contains 440 customers (observations) of a wholesale distributor. It includes the annual spend in monetary units on six product categories – **Fresh**, **Milk**, **Grocery**, **Frozen**, **Detergents_Paper**, and **Delicatessen**. We've created a new field called **Food** that includes all categories except **Detergents_Paper**, as shown in the following screenshot:

	A	B	C	D	E	F	G	H	I
1	Channel	Region	Fresh	Milk	Grocery	Frozen	Detergent	Delicasse	Food
2	2	3	12669	9656	7561	214	2674	1338	31438
3	2	3	7057	9810	9568	1762	3293	1776	29973
4	2	3	6353	8808	7684	2405	3516	7844	33094
5	1	3	13265	1196	4221	6404	507	1788	26874
6	2	3	22615	5410	7198	3915	1777	5185	44323
7	2	3	9413	8259	5126	666	1795	1451	24915

Load the new dataset into Rattle and go to the **Cluster** tab. Remember that, in unsupervised learning, there is no target variable.

I want to create a segmentation based only on buying behavior; for this reason, I set **Region** and **Channel** to **Ignore**, as shown here:

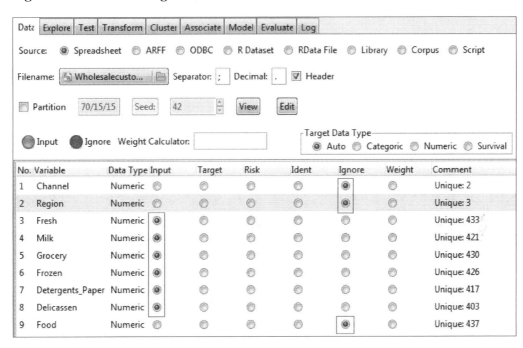

In the following screenshot, you can see the options Rattle offers for K-means. The most important one is **Number of clusters**; as we've seen, the analyst has to decide the number of clusters before running K-means:

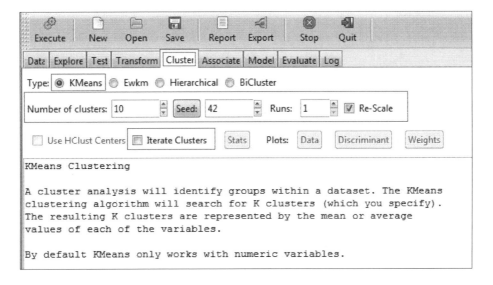

We have also seen that the initial position of the centroids can have some influence on the result of the algorithm. The position of the centroids is random, but we need to be able to reproduce the same experiment multiple times. When we're creating a model with K-means, we'll iteratively re-run the algorithm, tuning some options in order to improve the performance of the model. In this case, we need to be able to reproduce exactly the same experiment. Under the hood, R has a pseudo-random number generator based on a starting point called **Seed**. If you want to reproduce the exact same experiment, you need to re-run the algorithm using the same **Seed**.

Sometimes, the performance of K-means depends on the initial position of the centroids. For this reason, sometimes you need to able to re-run the model using a different initial position for the centroids. To run the model with different initial positions, you need to run with a different **Seed**.

After executing the model, Rattle will show some interesting information. The size of each cluster, the means of the variables in the dataset, the centroid's position, and the **Within cluster sum of squares** value. This measure, also called distortion, is the sum of the squared differences between each point and its centroid. It's a measure of the quality of the model.

Another interesting option is **Runs**; by using this option, Rattle will run the model the specified number of times and will choose the model with the best performance based on the **Within cluster sum of squares** value.

Deciding on the number of clusters can be difficult. To choose the number of clusters, we need a way to evaluate the performance of the algorithm. The sum of the squared distance between the observations and the associated centroid could be a performance measure. Each time we add a centroid to **KMeans**, the sum of the squared difference between the observations and the centroids decreases. The difference in this measure using a different number of centroids is the gain associated to the added centroids. Rattle provides an option to automate this test, called **Iterative Clusters**.

If you set the **Number of clusters** value to **10** and check the **Iterate Clusters** option, Rattle will run **KMeans** iteratively, starting with **3** clusters and finishing with **10** clusters. To compare each iteration, Rattle provides an iteration plot. In the iteration plot, the blue line shows the sum of the squared differences between each observation and its centroid. The red line shows the difference between the current sum of squared distances and the sum of the squared distance of the previous iteration. For example, for four clusters, the red line has a very low value; this is because the difference between the sum of the squared differences with three clusters and with four clusters is very small. In the following screenshot, the peak in the red line suggests that six clusters could be a good choice.

This is because there is an important drop in the **Sum of WithinSS** value at this point:

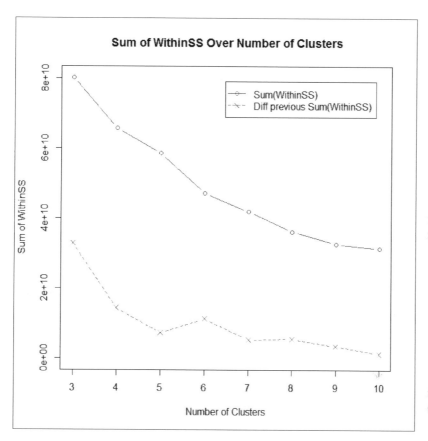

In this way, to finish my model, I only need to set the **Number of clusters** to **3**, uncheck the **Re-Scale** checkbox, and click on the **Execute** button:

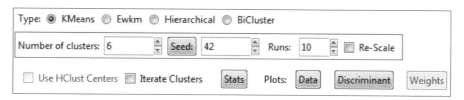

Finally, Rattle returns the six centroids of my clusters:

```
Cluster centers:

          Fresh      Milk   Grocery    Frozen  Detergents_Paper  Delicassen
1 46518.000  3438.682  4785.091  5249.955           801.0455    2147.227
2 20996.317  3826.433  5098.087  4157.010          1119.9423    1679.712
3 20031.286 38084.000 56126.143  2564.571         27644.5714    2548.143
4 60571.667 30120.333 17314.667 38049.333          2153.0000   20700.667
5  5996.482  3368.597  4206.765  2418.283          1282.9469    1001.305
6  5076.654 12288.526 18814.526  1605.000          8254.3974    1830.513
```

Now we have the six centroids and we want Rattle to associate each observation with a centroid. Go to the **Evaluate** tab, select the **KMeans** option, select the **Training** dataset, mark **All** in the report type, and click on the **Execute** button as shown in the following screenshot. This process will generate a CSV file with the original dataset and a new column called kmeans. The content of this attribute is a label (a number) representing the cluster associated with the observation (customer), as shown in the following screenshot:

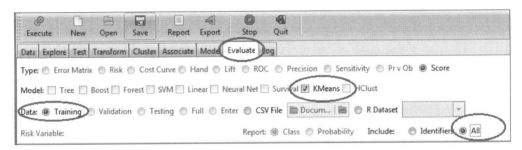

After clicking on the **Execute** button, you will need to choose a folder to save the resulting file to and will have to type in a filename. The generated data inside the CSV file will look similar to the following screenshot:

Customer_ID	Channel	Region	Fresh	Milk	Grocery	Frozen	Detergents_Paper	Delicassen	kmeans
1	2	3	12669	9656	7561	214	2674	1338	5
2	2	3	7057	9810	9568	1762	3293	1776	5
3	2	3	6353	8808	7684	2405	3516	7844	5
4	1	3	13265	1196	4221	6404	507	1788	2
5	2	3	22615	5410	7198	3915	1777	5185	2
6	2	3	9413	8259	5126	666	1795	1451	5
7	2	3	12126	3199	6975	480	3140	545	5
8	2	3	7579	4956	9426	1669	3321	2566	5
9	1	3	5963	3648	6192	425	1716	750	5
10	2	3	6006	11093	18881	1159	7425	2098	6

In the previous screenshot, you can see ten lines of the resulting file; note that the last column is kmeans.

Preparing the data in Qlik Sense

Our objective is to create the same data model that we created in *Chapter 4, Creating Your First Qlik Sense Application*, but using the new CSV file with the kmeans column. We have two options – we can reproduce all the steps we performed in the previous chapter to create a new application with the new file or we can update the Qlik Sense application we developed in the previous chapter.

We're going to update our application by replacing the customer data file with this new data file. Save the new file in the same folder as the original file, open the Qlik Sense application, and go to **Data load editor**.

There are two differences between the original file and this one. In the original file, we added a line to create a customer identifier called Customer_ID, and in this second file we have this field in the dataset. The second difference is that in this new file we have the **kmeans** column.

From **Data load editor**, go to the **Wholesale customer data** sheet, modify line 2, and add line 3. In line 2, we just load the content of Customer_ID, and in line 3, we load the content of the kmeans field and rename it to **Cluster**, as shown in the following screenshot. Finally, update the name of the file to be the new one and click on the **Load data** button:

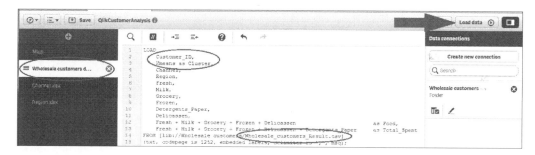

When the data load process finishes, open the data model viewer to check your data model, as shown here:

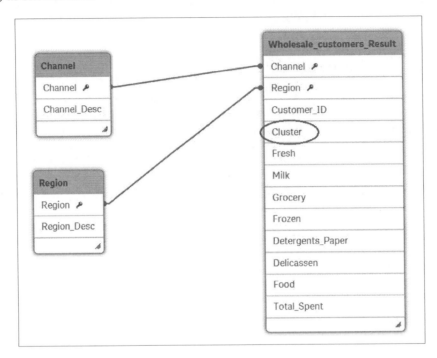

Note that you have the same data model with a new field called **Cluster**.

Creating a customer segmentation sheet in Qlik Sense

Now we can add a sheet to the application we developed in *Chapter 4, Creating Your First Qlik Sense Application*. We'll add three charts to see our clusters and how our customers are distributed in our clusters. The first chart will describe the buying behavior of each cluster, as shown here:

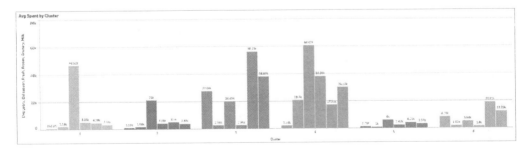

The second chart will show all customers distributed in a scatter plot, and in the last chart we'll see the number of customers that belong to each cluster, as shown here:

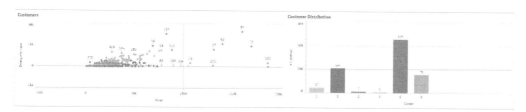

I'll start with the chart to the bottom-right; it's a bar chart with `Cluster` as the dimension and `Count([Customer_ID])` as the measure. This simple bar chart has something special – colors. Each customer's cluster has a special color code that we use in all charts. In this way, cluster **5** is blue in the three charts. To obtain this effect, we use this expression to define the color as `color(fieldindex('Cluster',` `Cluster))`, which is shown in the following screenshot:

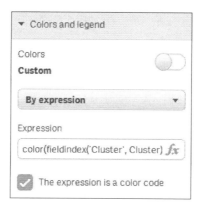

 You can find this color trick and more in this interesting blog by Rob Wunderlich – `http://qlikviewcookbook.com/`.

My second chart is the one at the top. I copied the previous chart and pasted it onto a free place. I kept the dimension but I changed the measure by using six new measures:

- `Avg([Detergents_Paper])`
- `Avg([Delicassen])`
- `Avg([Fresh])`
- `Avg([Frozen])`
- `Avg([Grocery])`
- `Avg([Milk])`

I placed my last chart at the bottom-left. I used a scatter plot to represent all of my 440 customers. I wanted to show the money spent by each customer on food and detergents, and its cluster. I used the *y* axis to show the money spent on detergents and the *x* axis for the money spent on food. Finally, I used colors to highlight the cluster. The dimension is `Customer_Id` and the measures are `Delicassen+Fresh+Fr ozen+Grocery+Milk` (or `Food`) and `[Detergents_Paper]`. As the final step, I reused the color expression from the earlier charts.

Now our first Qlik Sense application has two sheets – the original one is 100 percent Qlik Sense and helps us to understand our customers, channels, and regions. This new sheet uses clustering to give us a different point of view; this second sheet groups the customers by their similar buying behavior. All this information is useful to deliver better campaigns to our customers. Cluster **5** is our least profitable cluster, but is the biggest one with 227 customers. The main difference between cluster **5** and cluster **2** is the amount of money spent on fresh products. Can we deliver any offer to customers in cluster **5** to try to sell more fresh products?

Select retail customers and ask yourself, who are our best retail customers? To which cluster do they belong? Are they buying all our product categories?

Hierarchical clustering

Hierarchical clustering tries to group objects based on their similarity. To explain how this algorithm works, we're going to start with seven points (or observations) lying in a straight line:

We start by calculating the **distance** between each point. I'll come back later to the term distance; in this example, distance is the difference between two positions in the line. The points **D** and **E** are the ones with the smallest distance in between, so we group them in a cluster, as shown in this diagram:

Now, we substitute point **D** and point **E** for their mean (red point) and we look for the two points with the next smallest distance in between. In this second iteration, the closest points are **B** and **C**, as shown in this diagram:

We continue iterating until we've grouped all observations in the dataset, as shown here:

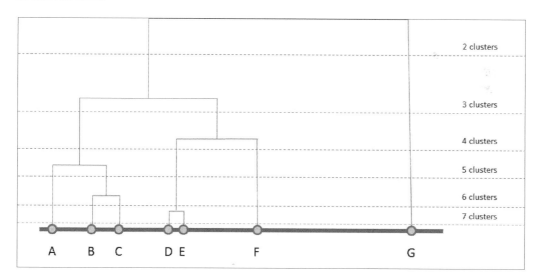

Note that, in this algorithm, we can decide on the number of clusters after running the algorithm. If we divide the dataset into two clusters, the first cluster is point **G** and the second cluster is **A, B, C, D, E**, and **F**. This gives the analyst the opportunity to see the big picture before deciding on the number of clusters.

The lowest level of clustering is a trivial one; in this example, seven clusters with one point in each one.

The chart I've created while explaining the algorithm is a basic form of a dendrogram. The **dendrogram** is a tree diagram used in Rattle and in other tools to illustrate the layout of the clusters produced by hierarchical clustering.

In the following screenshot, we can see the dendrogram created by Rattle for the wholesale customer dataset. In Rattle's dendrogram, the *y* axis represent all observations or customers in the dataset, and the *x* axis represents the distance between the clusters:

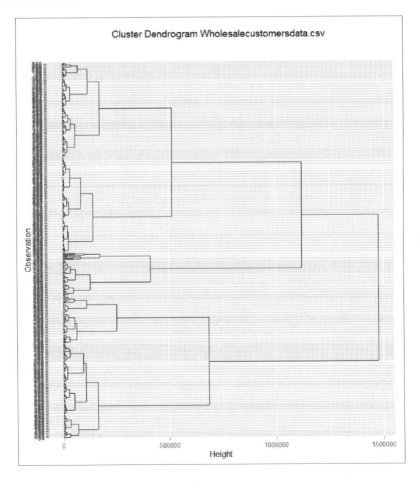

Association analysis

Association rules or association analysis is also an important topic in data mining. This is an unsupervised method, so we start with an unlabeled dataset. An **unlabeled dataset** is a dataset without a variable that gives us the right answer. Association analysis attempts to find relationships between different entities. The classic example of association rules is market basket analysis. This means using a database of transactions in a supermarket to find items that are bought together. For example, a person who buys potatoes and burgers usually buys beer. This insight could be used to optimize the supermarket layout.

Online stores are also a good example of association analysis. They usually suggest to you a new item based on the items you have bought. They analyze online transactions to find patterns in the buyer's behavior.

These algorithms assume all variables are categorical; they perform poorly with numeric variables. Association methods need a lot of time to be completed; they use a lot of CPU and memory. Remember that Rattle runs on R and the R engine loads all data into RAM memory.

Suppose we have a dataset such as the following:

Transaction 1	Burger	Chicken	Potatoes		
Transaction 2	Burger	Onions			
Transaction 3	Onions	Boots			
Transaction 4	Burger	Onions	Chicken		
Transaction 5	Burger	Onions	Chicken	Clothes	Potatoes
Transaction 6	Chicken	Clothes	Potatoes		
Transaction 7	Chicken	Potatoes	Clothes		

Our objective is to discover items that are purchased together. We'll create rules and we'll represent these rules like this:

$$Chicken, Potatoes \rightarrow Clothes$$

This rule means that when a customer buys **Chicken** and **Potatoes**, he tends to buy **Clothes**.

As we'll see, the output of the model will be a set of rules. We need a way to evaluate the quality or interest of a rule. There are different measures, but we'll use only a few of them. Rattle provides three measures:

- **Support**
- **Confidence**
- **Lift**

Support indicates how often the rule appears in the whole dataset. In our dataset, the rule Chicken, Potatoes → Clothes has a support of 48.57 percent (3 occurrences / 7 transactions).

Confidence measures how strong rules or associations are between items. In this dataset, the rule Chicken, Potatoes → Clothes has a confidence of **1**. The items Chicken and Potatoes appear three times in the dataset and the items Chicken, Potatoes, and Clothes appear three times in the dataset; and 3/3 = 1. A confidence close to **1** indicates a strong association.

In the following screenshot, I've highlighted the options on the **Associate** tab we have to choose from before executing an association method in Rattle:

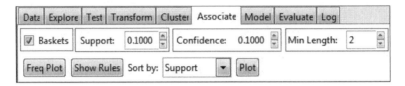

The first option is the **Baskets** checkbox. Depending on the kind of input data, we'll decide whether or not to check this option. If the option is checked, such as in the preceding screenshot, Rattle needs an identification variable and a target variable. After this example, we'll try another example without this option.

The second option is the minimum **Support** value; by default, it is set to `0.1`. Rattle will not return rules with a lower **Support** value than the one you have set in this text box. If you choose a higher value, Rattle will only return rules that appear many times in your dataset. If you choose a lower value, Rattle will return rules that appear in your dataset only a few times. Usually, if you set a high value for **Support**, the system will return only the obvious relationships. I suggest you start with a high **Support** value and execute the methods many times with a lower value in each execution. In this way, in each execution, new rules will appear that you can analyze.

The third parameter you have to set is **Confidence**. This parameter tells you how strong the rule is.

Finally, the length is the number of items that contains a rule. A rule like Beer è Chips has length of two. The default option for **Min Length** is 2. If you set this variable to 2, Rattle will return all rules with two or more items in it.

After executing the model, you can see the rules created by Rattle by clicking on the **Show Rules** button, as illustrated here:

Rattle provides a very simple dataset to test the association rules in a file called dvdtrans.csv. Test the dataset to learn about association rules.

Further learning

In this chapter, we introduced supervised and unsupervised learning, the two main subgroups of machine learning algorithms; if you want to learn more about machine learning, I suggest you complete a MOOC course called *Machine Learning* at Coursera:

https://www.coursera.org/learn/machine-learning

The acronym **MOOC** stands for **Massive Open Online Course**; these are courses open to participation via the Internet. These courses are generally free. Coursera is one of the leading platforms for MOOC courses.

Machine Learning is a great course designed and taught by Andrew Ng, Associate Professor at Stanford University; Chief Scientist at Baidu; and Chairman and Co-founder at Coursera. This course is really interesting.

A very interesting book is *Machine Learning with R* by Brett Lantz, *Packt Publishing*. This book contains a very interesting chapter about clustering and K-means with R.

Summary

In this chapter, we were introduced to machine learning, and supervised and unsupervised methods. We focused on unsupervised methods and covered centroid-based clustering, hierarchical clustering, and association rules.

We completed the application we started in *Chapter 4, Creating Your First Qlik Sense Application*. We used a simple dataset, but we saw how a clustering algorithm can complement a 100 percent Qlik Sense approach by adding more information.

In the next chapter, we'll cover supervised methods and we'll use decision trees as an example.

6

Decision Trees and Other Supervised Learning Methods

In the previous chapter, we introduced Machine Learning, unsupervised methods, and supervised methods. We focused on unsupervised learning and described some algorithms, we also concentrated on classifiers. We took time to study cluster analysis, focusing on centroids-based algorithms, and we also looked at hierarchical clustering.

We used Rattle to process customer data in order to create different clusters of customers, and then, we used Qlik Sense to visualize these different clusters.

The objective of this chapter is to introduce you to supervised learning. As I explained in the previous chapter, in supervised learning, the computer analyzes a set of examples to *learn* how to predict the output of a new situation.

We'll focus on Decision Tree Learning, or Decision Trees, because they're widely used and the knowledge *learned* by the tree is easy to translate to rules in any software, such as Qlik Sense. These rules are easy to understand for human experts.

In supervised learning, we split the dataset into three datasets — training, validation, and test. The training dataset usually contains 70 percent of the original observations, our algorithm will use this dataset in the training phase to *learn by example*. Each of the validation and test datasets usually contains 15 percent of the original observations. We'll use the validation dataset to fine-tune our algorithm, and finally, after the fine-tuning, we'll use the test dataset to evaluate the final performance of our algorithm. These three datasets match with the three phases of a supervised algorithm — training, validation (or tuning), and test (or performance evaluation).

In this chapter:

- We'll describe the main concepts of Decision Tree Learning.

- We'll review the algorithm and the possible applications, and we'll see examples based on these algorithms.

- Then, we'll use Rattle and Qlik Sense to create an application to classify new loan applications into low risk applications and high risk applications. We'll load that data into Qlik Sense and create a few example visualizations.

- After Decision Trees, we'll look at ensemble methods and Supported Vector Machines.

- Finally, we'll look at Neural Networks, which can be used as supervised or unsupervised learning and statistics methods such as Regression or Survival Analysis.

Partitioning datasets and model optimization

As we've explained, in supervised learning, we split the dataset in three subsets—training, validation, and testing:

To create the model or learner, Rattle uses the training dataset. After creating a model, we use the validation data to evaluate its performance. To improve the performance, depending on the algorithm we're using, we can use different tuning options. After tuning, we rebuild the model and evaluate its performance again. This is an iterative process; we create the model and evaluate it until we're fine with its performance.

For simplicity, in this chapter, we'll see only model creation, and in the following chapter, we'll see model optimization, but in real life, this is an iterative process.

The examples in this chapter will not have any optimization.

Finally, when you're happy with the model, you can use the testing dataset to confirm its performance. You need to use the testing dataset because you've used the validation dataset to optimize the model. You need to be sure that the optimizations you've done, work for all data, not just for the validation data.

Rattle splits the data randomly to assure that each dataset is representative, but when we optimize the model and test it again, we need to be able to repeat the same experiment exactly, with the same data. In this way, we'll be able to know if we're improving the model performance. To solve this problem, Rattle splits the dataset using a pseudo random number generator. Every time we split the dataset using the same **Seed**, we'll have the same subsets.

Decision Tree Learning

Decision Tree Learning uses past observations to learn how to classify them and also try to predict the class of a new observation. For example, in a bank, we may have historical information on the granting of loans. Usually, past loan information includes a customer profile and whether the customer defaulted or not. Based on this information, the algorithm can learn to predict whether a new customer will default.

We usually represent a Decision Tree as we did in the following diagram. The root node is at the top, and the leaves of the tree are at the bottom, the leaves represent a decision. In order to create rules from a tree, we need to start from the root node, and then we work downwards, towards the leaves. The following diagram represents a sample Decision Tree:

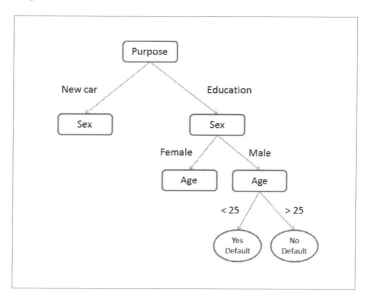

After studying the preceding diagram of a Decision Tree, we can obtain these rules:

```
If Purpose = 'Education' AND Sex = 'male' AND Age > 25 Then No
Default
If Purpose = 'Education' AND Sex = 'male' AND Age < 25 Then Yes
Default
```

As you can see, a tree is easy to translate to a set of *rules* or *If then* sentences. This is very useful for calculation by Rattle, or any other language, or system, such as Qlik Sense.

Finally, a human expert can understand the rules and the knowledge learned by the algorithm; in this way, a credit manager can understand and review why a computer has classified a loan application as dangerous or not dangerous.

In short, the main advantages of Decision Tree Learning are:

- The technique is simple
- It requires little data preparation
- The result is simple to understand for a human expert
- It is easy to visually represent

On the other hand, the main disadvantages are:

- **Unstable**: A little change in the input data can produce a big change in the output.
- **Overfitting**: Sometimes, Decision Tree Learners create very complex trees that do not generalize the data well. In other words, the algorithm learns how to classify the learning dataset, but fails to classify new observations.

Entropy and information gain

Before we explain how to create a Decision Tree, we need to introduce two important concepts—entropy and information gain.

Entropy measures the homogeneity of a dataset. Imagine a dataset with 10 observations with one attribute, as shown in the following diagram, the value of this attribute is **A** for the 10 observations. This dataset is completely homogenous and is easy to predict the value of the next observation, it'll probably be **A**:

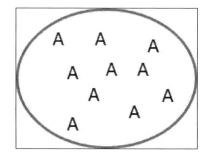

The entropy in a dataset that is completely homogenous is zero. Now, imagine a similar dataset, but in this dataset each observation has a different value, as shown in the following diagram:

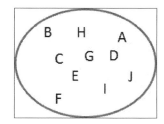

Now, the dataset is very heterogeneous and it's hard to predict the following observation. In this dataset, the entropy is higher. The formula to calculate the entropy is $Entropy = -\sum_i P_x \log_2 P_x$, where P_x is the probability of x.

Try to calculate the entropy for the following datasets:

$$E = -P_A * log_2 P_A = -\left(\frac{10}{10}\right) * log_2 \frac{10}{10} = 0$$

$$E = -(P_A * log_2 P_A + P_B * log_2 P_B) =$$
$$-\left(\left(\frac{5}{10}\right) * log_2 \frac{5}{10} + \left(\frac{5}{10}\right) * log_2 \frac{5}{10}\right) = 1$$

$$E = -(P_A * log_2 P_A + ... + P_J * log_2 P_J) = 3.32$$

Now, we understand how entropy helps us to know the level of predictability of a dataset. A dataset with a low entropy level is very predictable; a dataset with a high level of entropy is very hard to predict. We're ready to understand information gain and how entropy and information gain can help us to create a Decision Tree.

The **information gain** is a measure of the decrease of entropy you achieve when you split a dataset. We use it in the process of building a Decision Tree. We're going to use an example to understand this concept. In this example, our objective will be to create a tree to classify loan applications depending on its probability of defaulting, into low risk applications and high risk applications. Our dataset has three input variables: Purpose, Sex, and Age, and one output variable, Default?.

The following image shows the dataset:

Purpose	Sex	Age	Default?
New Car	Male	< 25	Yes
New Car	Male	25 - 65	No
New Car	Female	< 25	Yes
New Car	Female	25 - 65	Yes
New Car	Male	25 - 65	No
Education	Male	< 25	Yes
Education	Male	< 25	No
Education	Female	< 25	Yes
Education	Female	< 25	Yes
Education	Female	< 25	Yes
Vacations	Female	< 25	Yes
Vacations	Female	> 65	No
Vacations	Female	< 25	Yes
Vacations	Male	25 - 65	No
Vacations	Male	> 65	No

To create the Decision Tree, we will start by choosing an attribute for the root node. This attribute will split our dataset into two datasets. We will choose the attribute that adds more predictability or reduces the entropy. We will start calculating the entropy for the current dataset:

$$E = -\left(P_{yes} * log_2 P_{Yes} + P_{No} * log_2 P_{No}\right) = -\left(\frac{9}{15} * log_2 \frac{9}{15} + \frac{6}{15} * log_2 \frac{6}{15}\right) = 0.97$$

We will start with an entropy of 0.97; our objective is to try to reduce the entropy to increase the predictability. What happens if we choose the attribute Purpose for our root node? By choosing Purpose for our root node, we will divide the dataset in three datasets. Each dataset contains five observations. We can calculate the entropy of each dataset and aggregate it to have a global entropy value.

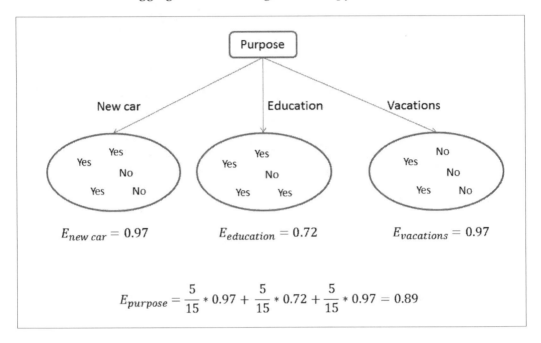

The original entropy was 0.97. If we use Purpose for our root node and divide the dataset into three sets, the entropy will be 0.89, so our new dataset will be more predictable. The difference between the original entropy and the new entropy is the information gain. In this example, the information gain is 0.08. However, what happens if we choose Sex or Age for our root node?

If we use Sex to split the dataset, we create two datasets. The male dataset contains seven observations and the female dataset contains eight observations; the new entropy is 0.91. In this case, the information gain is 0.06, so Purpose is a better option than Sex to split the dataset. Splitting the dataset by Purpose, the result becomes more predictable. This is illustrated in the following diagram:

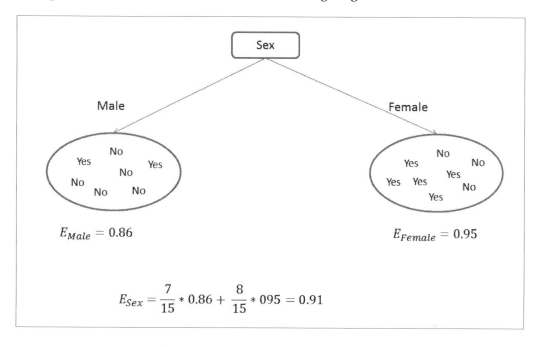

$$E_{Sex} = \frac{7}{15} * 0.86 + \frac{8}{15} * 095 = 0.91$$

Finally, if we use Age to split the dataset, we will obtain three subsets. The subset that contains young people (< 25) contains nine observations, the subset with middle-aged people contains four observations, and finally, the subset with people older than 65 years contains two observations. In this case, the entropy is 0.52 and the information gain is 0.45.

The attribute Age has the higher information gain; we will choose it for our root node, as illustrated in the following diagram:

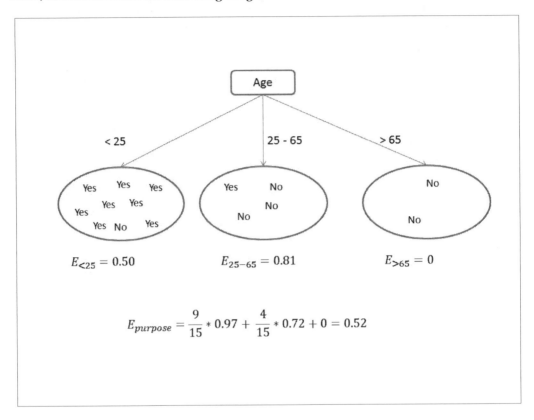

We've divided our dataset into three subsets, divided by Age.

After the root node, we need to choose a second attribute to split our three datasets and create a deeper tree.

Underfitting and overfitting

Underfitting and overfitting are problems not just with a classifier but for all supervised methods.

Imagine you have a classifier with just one rule that tries to distinguish between healthy and not healthy patients. The rule is as follows:

```
If Temperature < 37 then Healthy
```

This classifier will classify all patients with a lower temperature than 37 degrees, as healthy. This classifier will have a huge error rate. The tree that represents this rule will have only the root node and two branches, with a leaf in each branch.

Underfitting occurs when the tree is too short to classify a new observation correctly; the rules are too general.

On the other hand, if we have a dataset with many attributes, and if we generate a very deep Decision Tree, we risk the fact that our Tree fits well with the training dataset, but not able to predict new examples. In our previous example, we can have a rule such as this:

```
If Temperature<27 and Sintom_A = V …… and Sintom_B = Y …..Age=12
and … and Eyes = Blue and Height = 182 and Weight=74.6 then
Healthy
```

In this case, the rule is too specific. What happens if the weight of the next patient is 76? The classifier will not be able to classify the new patient correctly. The Tree is too deep and the rules are too specific; this problem is called **overfitting**. We'll see a very low error rate on training data, but a high error rate on test data.

We'll come back to overfitting in the next chapter.

Using a Decision Tree to classify credit risks

In this section, we will create a model to classify credit risks. In this section, we will create the model; we won't look at the performance of the model. We'll evaluate the performance of the model and improve it in the next chapter.

As we did before, to create this example, we'll download a dataset from the UCI Machine Learning Repository. We'll use a dataset called *Statlog (German Credit Data) Dataset*. The source of the dataset is Professor Dr. Hans Hofmann from Institut für Statistik und Ökonometrie, Universität Hamburg. The dataset classifies people described by a set of attributes as good or bad credit risks.

The dataset is downloaded from the following link:

```
https://archive.ics.uci.edu/ml/datasets/Statlog+%28German+Credit+Da
ta%29
```

In the following screenshot, you can see the original form of this dataset. The screenshot shows us the top ten lines of the dataset. The dataset doesn't have a header line. It contains 20 attributes, and the last column is the target variable—1 for Good Credit and 2 for Bad Credit. The attributes are separated by a blank space, as shown in this screenshot:

```
1   A11 6  A34 A43 1169 A65 A75 4 A93 A101 4 A121 67 A143 A152 2 A173 1 A192 A201 1
2   A12 48 A32 A43 5951 A61 A73 2 A92 A101 2 A121 22 A143 A152 1 A173 1 A191 A201 2
3   A14 12 A34 A46 2096 A61 A74 2 A93 A101 3 A121 49 A143 A152 1 A172 2 A191 A201 1
4   A11 42 A32 A42 7882 A61 A74 2 A93 A103 4 A122 45 A143 A153 1 A173 2 A191 A201 1
5   A11 24 A33 A40 4870 A61 A73 3 A93 A101 4 A124 53 A143 A153 2 A173 2 A191 A201 2
6   A14 36 A32 A46 9055 A65 A73 2 A93 A101 4 A124 35 A143 A153 1 A172 2 A192 A201 1
7   A14 24 A32 A42 2835 A63 A75 3 A93 A101 4 A122 53 A143 A152 1 A173 1 A191 A201 1
8   A12 36 A32 A41 6948 A61 A73 2 A93 A101 2 A123 35 A143 A151 1 A174 1 A192 A201 1
9   A14 12 A32 A43 3059 A64 A74 2 A91 A101 4 A121 61 A143 A152 1 A172 1 A191 A201 1
10  A12 30 A34 A40 5234 A61 A71 4 A94 A101 2 A123 28 A143 A152 2 A174 1 A191 A201 2
```

We prefer to work with a CSV file with a header line and the attributes separated by commas. For this reason, before loading the dataset into Rattle, we work it a little, with a spreadsheet editor, to transform the original file.

To label each column, we used the following information document provided with the dataset:

Column	Label	Values
1	Status of existing checking account	A11:... < 0 DM
		A12: 0 <= ... < 200 DM
		A13: ... >= 200 DM/salary assignments for at least 1 year
		A14: no checking account
2	Duration in months	Numeric
3	Credit history	A30: no credits taken/all credits paid back duly
		A31: all credits at this bank paid back duly
		A32: existing credits paid back duly till now
		A33: delay in paying off in the past
		A34: critical account/other credits existing (not at this bank)

Column	Label	Values
4	Purpose	A40: car (new)
		A41: car (used)
		A42: furniture/equipment
		A43: radio/television
		A44: domestic appliances
		A45: repairs
		A46: education
		A47: (vacation - does not exist?)
		A48: retraining
		A49: business
		A410: others
5	Credit amount	Numeric
6	Savings account/bonds	A61: ... < 100 DM
		A62: 100 <= ... < 500 DM
		A63: 500 <= ... < 1000 DM
		A64: >= 1000 DM
		A65: unknown/ no savings account
7	Present employment since	A71: unemployed
		A72: ... < 1 year
		A73: 1 <= ... < 4 years
		A74: 4 <= ... < 7 years
		A75: .. >= 7 years
8	Installment rate in percentage of disposable income	Numeric
9	Personal status and sex	A91: male: divorced/separated
		A92: female: divorced/separated/ married
		A93: male : single
		A94: male: married/widowed
		A95: female: single
10	Other debtors/ guarantors	A101: none
		A102: co-applicant
		A103: guarantor

Column	Label	Values
11	Present residence since	Numeric
12	Property	A121: real estate A122: if not A121: building society savings agreement/life insurance A123: if not A121/A122: car or other, not in attribute 6 A124: unknown/no property
13	Age in years	Numeric
14	Other installment plans	A141: bank A142: stores A143: none
15	Housing	A151: rent A152: own A153: for free
16	Number of existing credits at this bank	Numeric
17	Job	A171: unemployed/unskilled - non-resident A172: unskilled - resident A173: skilled employee/official A174: management/self-employed/ highly qualified employee/ officer
18	Number of people being liable to provide maintenance for	Numeric
19	Telephone	A191: none A192: yes, registered under the customers name
20	foreign worker	A201: yes A202: no
21	Target	1: Good 2: Bad

To create our classifier, we will start by loading the data into Rattle and identifying the target variable. During the data load, we'll split the dataset into three datasets—the training dataset, the validation dataset, and the testing dataset. As we've explained in this chapter, we'll use the training dataset to create our model, the validation dataset to tune it, and the testing dataset to evaluate the final performance. We'll come back to this in the next chapter when we look at cross-validation. The following screenshot shows how to split the original dataset into three datasets:

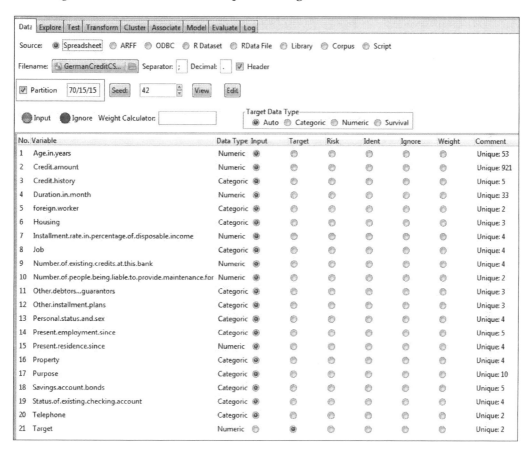

To create a Decision Tree, after loading the credit data, go to the **Model** tab. In this section, we will use **Tree**. We'll see the other models later in this chapter.

In the following screenshot, we can see that, to create a Decision Tree, Rattle offers us two algorithms, traditional and conditional. The traditional algorithm works as we've seen in this chapter. The conditional algorithm helps to address overfitting; this algorithm can work better than the traditional algorithm in many cases. To optimize our Tree, Rattle has six parameters. As we'll see in the next chapter, one of the most common problems of supervised learning is overfitting; these parameters will help us to avoid it by reducing the complexity of the resulting Tree:

- **Min Split**: This is the minimum number of observations needed to create a new branch.

- **Min Bucket**: This is the minimum number of observations in each leaf.

- **Max Depth**: This is the maximum depth of the tree.

- **Complexity**: With this parameter, we will control the minimum *gain* needed to create a new branch. If the value is high, the resulting tree will be simple; if the value is low, the resulting tree will be more complex.

- **Priors**: Sometimes, the distribution of the target variable doesn't match with the real distribution. Imagine a dataset with a lot of sick patients. We can use this parameter to inform Rattle of the correct distribution of the target variable.

- **Loss Matrix**: In the next chapter, we'll see that in some cases, we need to distinguish between different kinds of misclassifications or errors. This parameter will help us to address this problem.

Finally, we've two important buttons: **Rules** and **Draw**. We will use these buttons just after creating our first tree, as shown here:

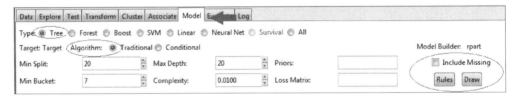

Set the following parameters as in the previous screenshot and press **Execute**:

- **Min Split**; 20
- **Max Depth**: 20
- **Min Bucket**: 7
- **Complexity**: 0.0100

Rattle will create a tree and will show the new tree in the screen. In the following screenshot, we've shown the root node and the first two branches of the tree:

```
Summary of the Decision Tree model for Classification (built using 'rpart'):

n= 700

node), split, n, loss, yval, (yprob)
      * denotes terminal node

 1) root 700 209 1 (0.70142857 0.29857143)
   2) Status.of.existing.checking.account=A13,A14 326   44 1 (0.86503067 0.13496933) *
   3) Status.of.existing.checking.account=A11,A12 374 165 1 (0.55882353 0.44117647)
```

In the second line, n= 700 is the size of the training set. Remember that our original dataset has 1,000 observations, but we've divided the complete dataset into training (70 percent), validation (15 percent), and testing (15 percent). For this reason, the size of the training dataset is 700.

In the fifth line, we see the root node. The number 1) is the node; root denotes that this is the root node; 700 is the number of observations; 209 is the number of observations misclassified, 1 is the default value for the target variable, and (0.70142857 0.29857143) is the distribution of the target variable. In our example, 0.7014 of the observations are classified as 1 (good credit risk) and 0.2986 are classified as 2 (bad credit risk).

```
1) root 700 209 1 (0.70142857 0.29857143)
```

The following lines show us the second and third nodes:

```
2) Status.of.existing.checking.account=A13,A14 326   44 1 (0.86503067
0.13496933) *
3) Status.of.existing.checking.account=A11,A12 374 165 1 (0.55882353
0.44117647)
```

In this node, the symbol * in the second node indicates that it's a leaf. The attribute Status.of.existing.checking.account is used by Rattle to create a branch. If the value of this attribute is A13 (>= 200 DM/salary assignments for at least 1 year) or A14 (no checking account), the observation belongs to the second node. This second node is a leaf with 326 observations classified as 1 (good credit risk) and 44 observations are misclassified.

If the value of the attribute is `A11` (`... < 0 DM`) or `A12` (`0 <= ... < 200 DM`), the observation belongs to the third node. This node has 374 observations, but it's not a leaf node, so under this node, we'll have more branches.

Now, press the **Draw** button, and you'll have a graphical representation of the same tree, as shown here:

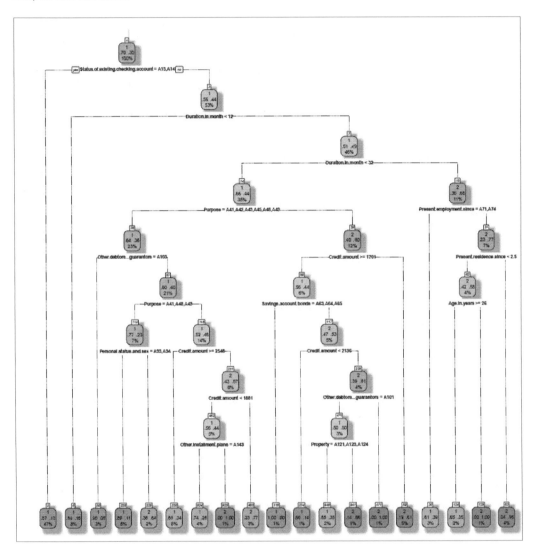

As we've seen, one advantage of trees is that it is easy to convert trees into rules that are easy to translate to other languages such as SQL, or Qlik Sense. Now push the **Rules** button to create the set of rules.

In our example, Rattle generates 19 rules. In the next chapter we'll see how to evaluate the performance of this model. Now, we'll focus on understanding the rules and how to use them. In the following screenshot, we see the first rule:

```
==================================================================
Tree as rules:

 Rule number: 125 [Target=2 cover=9 (1%) prob=1.00]
    Status.of.existing.checking.account=A11,A12
    Duration.in.month>=11.5
    Duration.in.month>=31.5
    Present.employment.since=A72,A73,A75
    Present.residence.since< 2.5
    Age.in.years< 26.5
```

The rule we see in the previous screenshot is the rule number 125. There are 9 observations that fall into this rule (cover=9); these 9 observations are 1 percent of the dataset. When an observation falls under this rule, the probability that the value of the target variable is I 2 (Target=2), is 1.0 (prob=1.0).

This rule looks very specific because it fits perfectly into a small number of observations; we'll improve it in the following chapter.

Using Rattle to score new loan applications

As we've explained before, we will call scores to the process of predicting the output for new examples. We've two options to score new observations with our Decision Tree; we can code the Decision Tree rules in Qlik Sense or we can use Rattle to automatically score new observations.

As you have seen before, the rules are easy to translate to an *If then* structure that is easy to implement in any language. Imagine Rattle provides you with a set of 10 rules and the first rule is as follows:

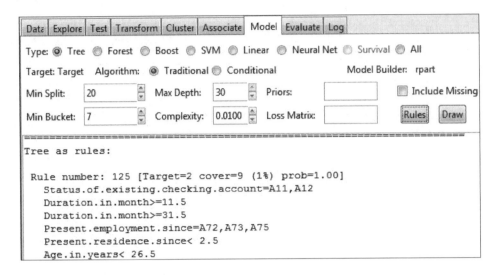

In the following screenshot, we see how we can create a new attribute called Prediction. In this example, we will just see the implementation of the rule 109 using the Qlik Sense **Data load editor**, but we can use the *If then* structures to implement all the rules, as shown here:

```
// Rule number: 125 [Target=2 cover=9 (1%) prob=1.00]
if (("Status of existing checking account" = 'A11' OR "Status of existing checking account" = 'A12') AND
    ("Duration in month">=11.5 AND "Duration in month">=31.5) AND
    ("Present residence since" = 'A72' OR "Present residence since" = 'A73' OR "Present residence since" = 'A75') AND
    ( "Present residence since" < 2.5) AND
    ("Age in years" < 26.5), 2, 0) AS Prediction,
```

Now, we have a new attribute in our table called Prediction that gives us a prediction for the credit risk.

Rattle provides us an option to automatically score new observations. Using this option, we don't need to manually code the rules; for this reason, we will use Rattle to score new credit applications in this example.

In the Rattle's **Evaluate** tab, there are different types of evaluation. In this section, we will use **Score**, as shown in the following screenshot. Under the type of evaluation, there is the model we will use. In our example, we've only built a Tree model, for this reason, we will choose **Tree**.

Under the model, we must choose the data we want to score. The two most usual options are **Testing** and **CSV File**. We can score new observations contained in a CSV file by selecting the **CSV File** option. In our example, we will use the **Testing** option to score the testing:

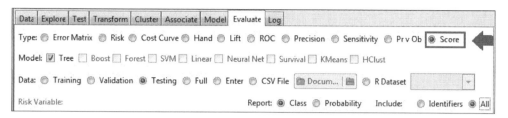

Finally, we have to choose the type of report we want to create. Choose **Class** and a category will be created for each observation. In the **Include** option, choose **All** to include all variables in the report. Press the **Execute** button and Rattle will create a CSV file with all original variables and a new one called `rpart`, as shown in this screenshot:

	Account.S	Duration	Credit.His	Purpose	Amount	Savings.	Present.e	Instalmen	status.and	Other.del	Present.r	Property	Age	Other.ins	Housing	Number.c	Job	Number.c	Phone	foreign.w	Target	rpart
2	A14	12	A32	A43	3059	A64	A74	2	A91	A101	4	A121	61	A143	A152	1	A172	1	A191	A201	1	1
3	A11	30	A30	A49	8072	A65	A72	2	A93	A101	3	A123	25	A141	A152	3	A173	1	A191	A201	1	1
4	A12	24	A32	A41	12579	A61	A75	4	A92	A101	2	A124	44	A143	A153	1	A174	1	A192	A201	2	2
5	A11	6	A32	A42	1374	A61	A73	1	A93	A101	2	A121	36	A141	A152	1	A172	1	A192	A201	1	1
6	A12	18	A32	A49	1913	A64	A72	3	A94	A101	3	A121	36	A141	A152	1	A173	1	A192	A201	1	1
7	A14	12	A34	A43	1264	A65	A75	4	A93	A101	4	A124	57	A143	A151	1	A172	1	A191	A201	1	1
8	A14	36	A32	A43	2299	A63	A75	4	A93	A101	4	A123	39	A143	A152	1	A173	1	A191	A201	1	1

Now, we have a file containing all the variables of the testing dataset and a prediction for each observation. In the next section, we will use Qlik Sense to create a visual application for the business user. With this application, the business users will be able to access new applications information.

Creating a Qlik Sense application to predict credit risks

In the previous section, we've created a Decision Tree using Rattle and we've scored the testing dataset using the model we created. In this section, we'll use Qlik Sense to build a visual application to explore new loan applications.

The German Credit dataset contains two different types of input variables, numeric, and categorical. In a categorical variable such as `Purpose`, each observation contains a value, and possible values for `Purpose` are A40, A41, A42, A43, A44, and A45. Each value has meaning, for example A40 means a new car. In order to help the user to understand and explore the data, we want to translate all categorical values to its meaning. Like in *Chapter 4, Creating Your First Qlik Sense Application*, we'll add a description in separate tables and we'll build a data model, such as the following screenshot:

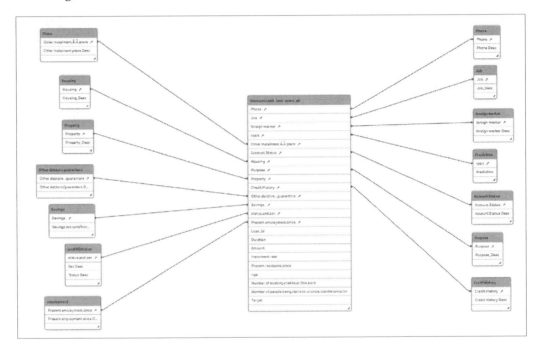

Remember that to link two tables, Qlik Sense needs two fields with exactly the same names.

Now, we need to create a table for each categorical variable containing the original value and its translation. For the variable `Purpose`, we'll create a table like the following:

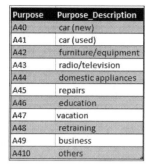

Purpose	Purpose_Description
A40	car (new)
A41	car (used)
A42	furniture/equipment
A43	radio/television
A44	domestic appliances
A45	repairs
A46	education
A47	vacation
A48	retraining
A49	business
A410	others

Use a spreadsheet tool such as Microsoft Excel, to create a file that contains a sheet for each categorical variable.

Now, we've two files with one file containing the scored testing dataset, and a file with all the descriptions for the categorical variables.

You've learned in *Chapter 4*, *Creating Your First Qlik Sense Application*, about how to load data into Qlik Sense. In this example, we have a file with 14 sheets or tables. If you want to load all sheets, you can select all sheets in the data load wizard, like in the following screenshot:

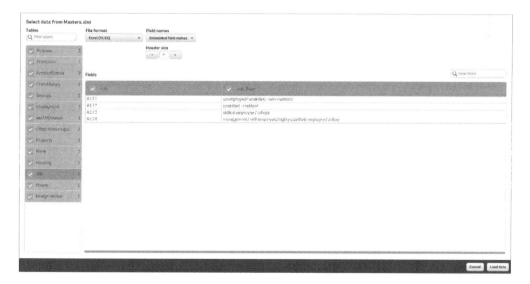

After loading the data, we create a visual application for the business user. You've learned in *Chapter 4, Creating Your First Qlik Sense Application*, and, *Chapter 5, Clustering and Other Unsupervised Learning Methods*, on how to create this application. One benefit of Qlik Sense is that it gives self-service data visualization; it means that each user can create his own charts depending on his interests. You can create the application you want; as an example, we've created an application with two sheets. The first sheet is an overview and the second sheet contains a table to see all the details of new applications, as shown in the following screenshot:

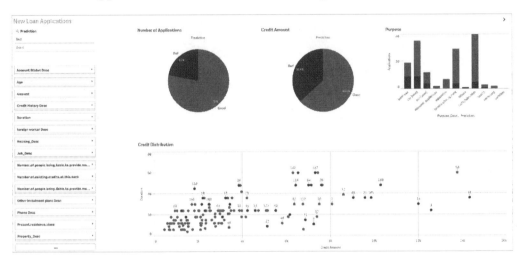

Ensemble classifiers

Thomas G Dietterich defines Ensemble methods as follows:

> *"Ensemble methods are learning algorithms that construct a set of classifiers and then classify new data points by taking a (weighted) vote of their prediction."*

You can get more information from http://web.engr.oregonstate.edu/~tgd/publications/mcs-ensembles.pdf.

Ensemble methods create a set of weak classifiers and combine them into a strong classifier. A weak classifier is a classifier that performs slightly better than a classifier that randomly guesses the prediction. Rattle offers two types of ensemble models: Random Forest and Boosting.

Boosting

Boosting is an ensemble method, so it creates a set of different classifiers. Imagine that you have m classifiers, we can define a classifier x as:

$$Tree_x(new\ observation) = Classification_x$$

When we need to evaluate a new observation, we can calculate the average of all m tree's predictions using the following formula:

$$Tree(new\ observation) = \frac{\sum_{i=1}^{m} Tree_i(new\ observation)}{m}$$

We can improve this evaluation by adding a weight to each tree, as shown here in this formula:

$$Tree(new\ observation) = \sum_{i=1}^{m} Weight_i * Tree_i(new\ observation)$$

We can use this mechanism for Regression and also for classification (for example, if the result is higher or equal to one, the observation belongs to class X). For classification, we can also use other mechanisms such as the majority of vote.

Now, we know to ensemble a set of classifiers, but we need to create this set of classifiers. To create different classifiers, we will use different subsets of data.

The most usual boosting algorithm is AdaBoost or adaptive boosting. This algorithm was created by Yoav Freund and Robert Schapire in 1997. In AdaBoost, we start by assigning equal weights to all observations. To create the first tree, we will select a random set of observations. After creating and evaluating the model, we will increase the weight of misclassified observations in order to *boost* misclassified observations. Now, we can create the second leaner or model by selecting a new random set of observations. After creating each leaner, we will increase the weight of misclassified observations.

To create a boosting model, you have to go to Rattle's **Model** tab and select the **Boost** type, as shown in the following screenshot:

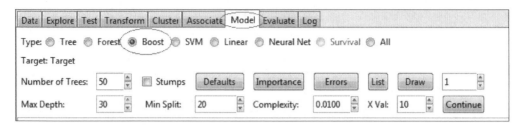

Rattle offers different options, the most important ones are:

- **Number of Trees**: This is the number of different trees the algorithm will ensemble
- **Max Depth**: This is the maximum depth of the final tree
- **Min Split**: In the **Tree** option, this is the minimum number of observations needed to create a new branch
- **Complexity**: In the **Tree** option, this parameter controls the minimum gain in terms of complexity needed to create a new branch

In an ensemble algorithm, **Out-Of-Bag Error** or OOB Error is a good approach to performance. OOBs are observations that are not in the subset used to create each tree. Rattle uses all observations that aren't in the subset used to create the trees to validate the model. When we see an OOB Error of 0.123, it means that our model correctly classifies 87.7 percent of the observation that wasn't in the random training set.

When we execute the Boost model, Rattle returns information in text form. See highlighted in the following screenshot, the **Out-of-Bag Error** and **iteration** values. In our example, the iteration is 46. We ran the example with the variable **Number of Trees** set to 46; a iteration of 46 and OOB error 0.123 means that with 46 trees, we can achieve a OOB error of 0.123. If we increase the **Number of Trees** value to 50, we won't be able to achieve a better OOB Error, as shown here:

```
Summary of the Ada Boost model:

Call:
ada(Target ~ ., data = crs$dataset[crs$train, c(crs$input, crs$target)],
    control = rpart.control(maxdepth = 30, cp = 0.01, minsplit = 20,
        xval = 10), iter = 50)

Loss: exponential Method: discrete    Iteration: 50

Final Confusion Matrix for Data:
          Final Prediction
True value   1    2
         1 481   10
         2  54  155

Train Error: 0.091

Out-Of-Bag Error:   0.123   iteration= 46
```

If you press the button; **Errors**, Rattle will plot the OOB Error, and you will see how it evolves when you add more trees to the model.

Finally, we've created a set of trees; we can see each tree in the text format or as a plot by pushing the **List** or **Draw** button and select the number of trees in the text field, as shown here:

Random Forest

Random Forest is an ensemble method developed by *Leo Breiman* and *Adele Cutler* in 2001. This is an ensemble algorithm, so we don't have a single tree, we've a set of trees or a forest. Random Forest combines this set of trees in a single model to improve the performance.

The main idea is to produce a set of trees, introducing some randomness in each tree, and combine all of them to produce a better prediction. The randomness is produced in two different ways; in the set of variables used to split the data in branches, and in the observations used to create (train) the tree.

The basic algorithm, is the same as we've already seen in this chapter, but now we will create a fixed number of trees. We need to decide the **Number of Trees** value and Rattle will create this many number of trees for us. Before it creates a tree, it randomly selects a set of observations to train the classifier and uses a randomly chosen subset of input variables to split the data. The final result is a set of trees.

In order to predict a new observation, Random Forest evaluates the new observations for each tree. If the target attribute is categorical (classification), Random Forest will choose the most frequent as its prediction. If the target variable is numerical (Regression), the average of all predictions will be chosen.

To create a Random Forest model in Rattle, you have to load a dataset, go to the **Model** tab, and choose **Forest** as the model type, as shown here:

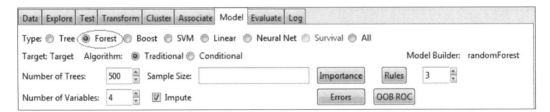

After selecting **Forest** as the model type, press the **Execute** button to create the model. After executing Random Forest, Rattle creates a summary. The summary contains the following:

- The number of observations used to train the model
- Whether the model includes observations with missing values
- The type of trees—Classification or Regression

- The number of trees created
- The number of variables used at each split
- The OOB estimate of the error rate
- The confusion matrix

We'll see the confusion matrix in the next chapter. Now, we have to see the OOB estimate of the error rate. In the following screenshot, we will see 23 percent as the **OOB estimate of error rate**. This rate is high, and means our model has low performance, as indicated in this screenshot:

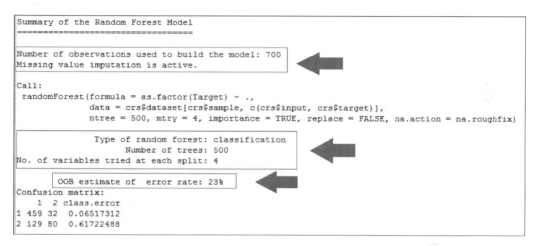

```
Summary of the Random Forest Model
==================================

Number of observations used to build the model: 700
Missing value imputation is active.

Call:
 randomForest(formula = as.factor(Target) ~ .,
              data = crs$dataset[crs$sample, c(crs$input, crs$target)],
              ntree = 500, mtry = 4, importance = TRUE, replace = FALSE, na.action = na.roughfix)

                Type of random forest: classification
                      Number of trees: 500
No. of variables tried at each split: 4

        OOB estimate of  error rate: 23%
Confusion matrix:
    1  2 class.error
1 459 32  0.06517312
2 129 80  0.61722488
```

Rattle offers you some options to improve the model. You can choose **Number of Trees** that the model will create and **Number of Variables;** in between, Rattle will choose one to split the dataset. We can use the **Impute** checkbox to control whether observations with missing values are ignored or not.

We've four buttons: **Importance**, **Rules**, **Errors** and **OOB ROC**. You've seen before that by pressing the **Rules** button, Rattle converts a tree to a set of rules. In this case, we have a set of trees. For this reason, we've a text field where we can indicate the number of trees. If we write three in the text field and press **Rules**, Rattle will convert the tree number three, to a set of rules.

The **Importance** button creates a plot that shows two measures of the variable importance prediction accuracy and Gini index. The Gini index is a measure of the inequality of a distribution. These two measures help us to understand which variables are more useful for predicting a new observation.

There is a trade-off between the error rate and the time needed to create the model. If we choose to create a small number of trees, Rattle will need a small amount of time to create it, but the error rate will be high. If we choose creating a large number of trees, the time needed will be higher, but the error rate will be lower. A good tool to choose the number of trees is the error plot. Press the **Error** button and Rattle will create an error plot. This plot shows us the evolution of the OOB estimate of error rate when you increase the number of trees. Look at the following screenshot; when the number of trees is small, the error rate is high; by incrementing the number of trees, we will decrease the error rate. In the same plot, we can see the error rate associated with each prediction:

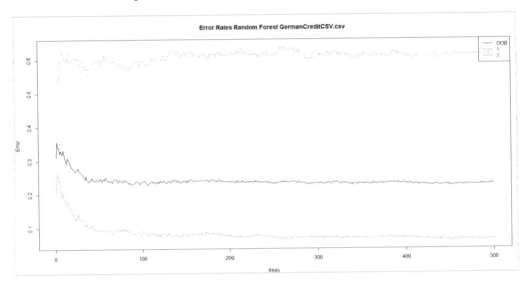

Finally, **Sample Size** can be used to limit the number of observations necessary to create each tree, or in a classifier, can be used to define the number of observations of each class that will be used. In our credit example, we've 1,000 observations; 700 are classified as 1, and 300 are classified as 2. On average, the number of observations classified as 1 in each sample dataset will be 70 percent. We can use **Sample Size** to create a different distribution. If you use 200,200 as the **Sample Size** value, each sample dataset will contain 200 observations classified as 1 and 200 as 2.

Supported Vector Machines

Supported Vector Machine (SVM) is a supervised method used for Classification and Regression. SVM looks for the *best separation* between observations that belong to different classes. The best separation is the one with the higher margin. In the following diagram, you can see a dataset with two classes of observations: stars and circles. On the left-hand side, the observations are divided by a line called **Line 1**. On the right-hand side, there is the same dataset divided by a line called **Line 2**:

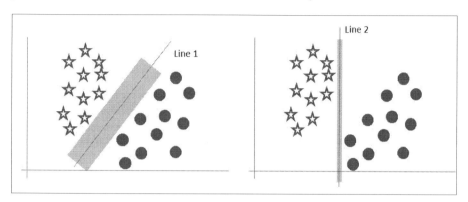

In this example, our dataset only has two attributes and can be represented in a plane and divided by a simple line, but usually our datasets are more complex and have a lot of attributes. We need to use a hyperplane to divide them.

Usually, different classes in a dataset are not easily separable as on our previous example. For this reason, *Kernel Functions* are used to preprocess the attributes of the observations to convert into easier separable observations. The performance of the model depends on the Kernel Function used.

Other models

In this section, we will see other models provided by Rattle in the **Model** tab, which aren't supervised learning. These methods are Linear and Logistic Regression, Neural Networks, and Survival Analysis.

Linear and Logistic Regression

Linear Regression is a statistical method to describe the relationship between one or more input variables and one or more output variables. The objective is to create a formula that models the relationships between input and output variables; in this way, we can use this formula to predict new observations.

Imagine you are the manager of a marina, your marina has a gas station and you need to predict the amount of gas oil you will sell during a summer day. On the Mediterranean coast, during the summer, the amount of gas oil sold is correlated to the temperature. The reason is obvious, on sunny days, the temperature rises and more tourists want to use their boats. The example is illustrated in this diagram:

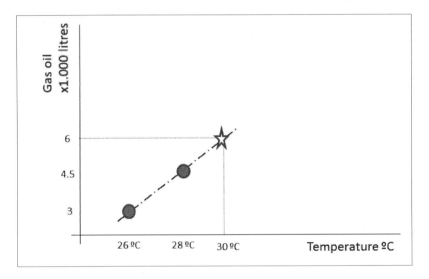

Based on past experience, we know that on a day with a temperature of 26°C, the gas station sold 3,000 liters, and on a 28°C day, it sold 4,500 liters. In this example, we can assume that the relationship between **Gas oil Sold** and **Temperature** is described by this equation:

$$Gas\ oil\ Sold = a + b * Temperature$$

This equation describes the relationship between Gas oil Sold and Temperature. Using this equation and a weather forecast, we can predict the gas oil our gas station will sell tomorrow.

When our dataset has one output variable, we will call it **Simple Linear Regression**. If we have more than one output variable, we call it **Multiple Linear Regression**.

We use Linear Regression when the target variable is numerical. In classification tasks, when the target variable is categorical, we will use Logistic Regression. When the target variable has two possible values or classes, we can use binary or binomial Logistic Regression.

Neural Networks

The Neural Network model is a method that can be used as supervised or unsupervised learning. Neural Networks are especially useful for pattern recognition and time series prediction; real-world applications include facial recognition, character recognition, or stock prices.

Neural Networks are inspired by the human brain and have three main layers:

- **Input Layer**: This layer receives the input data and passes them to the hidden layer.

- **Hidden Layer**: This layer contains a number of interconnected nodes. These nodes, called neurons, are mathematical functions that create the predictions.

- **Output Layer**: This layer creates the final prediction from the predictions done in the hidden layer.

Neural Networks work especially well, when the number of input or attributes in the observations is high. An important disadvantage of Neural Networks is that the Hidden Layer is a black box and the algorithm doesn't explain the value of the prediction.

Further learning

You can find a great introduction to Data Science in *Introduction to Data Science*, a very interesting Coursera course. The instructor is Bill Howe, Director of Research Scalable Data Analytics at the University of Washington. You can find more details from the following location:

```
https://www.coursera.org/course/datasci
```

The course has a very interesting section about Machine Learning. In this section, you will find a very intuitive introduction to entropy, information gain, and Decision Tree Learning.

In the last chapter, we've referenced *Machine Learning with R, Brett Lantz, Packt Publishing*. In this book, you can find a section about Decision Trees and the author develops an example using the German Credit dataset.

Summary

In this chapter, we've seen the concept of entropy and information gain. We've learned to create a Decision Tree with these concepts. After this, we've used Rattle to create a model to predict credit risk. We've translated our tree to rules, and seen how to code them in Qlik Sense.

After Decision Trees, we saw how ensemble models combine a set of learners to create a better model. We've focused on two ensemble models: Random Forest and Boosting.

Then, we've introduced Supported Vector Machines, and finally, we've covered other methods such as Regression and Neural Networks.

During this entire chapter, we didn't worry about the model performance, we just created the models. However, we avoided looking at the prediction accuracy of all these different models. In the next chapter, we'll learn how to compare the performance of different models and see how to optimize a model.

In real life, model creation and optimization are iterative processes. You can create a model and evaluate its performance. Then, you have to test different model parameters, evaluate the performance again, and compare the new performance with your previous performance. In this book, model creation and optimization are split into different chapters for simplicity.

7
Model Evaluation

In the previous chapter, we've seen how to create supervised learning methods. We divided our datasets into three subsets—**training**, **validation**, and **testing**. We also used the training dataset to train our models, and in this chapter, we'll use the validation dataset to measure the model performance and to compare different models.

In this chapter, we'll explore different methods for measuring the predictive power of a model.

As we've seen before, there are two kinds of predictive models: regression and classification. In a regression model, the output variable is a numeric variable; in a classification model, the output variable is a categorical variable. We'll start this chapter with cross-validation. After this, we'll measure the performance in regression methods, and then, we'll move on to classification performance.

Cross-validation

Cross-validation is a very useful technique to evaluate the performance of a supervised method. We will randomly split our dataset into k sub-datasets called folds (usually, 5 to 10). We will choose a fold for testing and keep the rest for training. We will train the model using the other $k-1$ folds and test it with a fold. We will repeat this process of training and testing k times, each time keeping a different folder for testing.

In each iteration, we will create a model and obtain a performance measure such as accuracy. When we've finished, we have k measures of performance, and we can obtain the performance of the modeling technique by calculating the average.

Using Rattle, we can split the original dataset into training, validation, and testing. Some R packages implement cross-validation when creating the model. If the model we are creating, uses cross-validation, we can skip the creation of the validation dataset and only create the training and testing datasets.

When we build a tree, such as in the previous chapter, Rattle uses the RPART package. This package implements cross-validation. For this reason, after building the model, the last information that Rattle gives us is the complexity table, which is shown here:

```
Root node error: 209/700 = 0.29857

n= 700

          CP nsplit  rel error   xerror      xstd
1 0.036683      0    1.00000  1.00000  0.057932
2 0.023923      4    0.80861  0.99522  0.057852
3 0.016746      6    0.76077  0.93780  0.056839
4 0.012759      8    0.72727  0.96172  0.057273
5 0.011962     14    0.61244  0.96651  0.057358
6 0.010000     18    0.56459  0.96651  0.057358
```

In the complexity table, we can see the **Complexity Parameter (CP)** that we've discussed in the previous chapter, the number of splits (**nsplit**), the error in the training set (**error**), and the cross-validated error (**xerror**). Notice that by incrementing the number of splits, we will reduce the error on the training dataset very fast, but we're not interested in that because a low error in the training dataset doesn't assure a low error with the new observation. We want to reduce the cross-validated error. We can see that on row **3** with **6** folds, we've the lowest cross-validated error; after row **3**, the error increases. For this reason, Rattle stops splitting the dataset.

Regression performance

To measure the performance of a regression, the distance between the predicted outputs and the actual outputs, is a good model performance measure.

Rattle offers us a good way to see predicted values versus the actual value—the Predicted versus Observed plot. To test this plot, you need to create a regression model. You can download a sample dataset from the **UCI Machine Learning Repository** (http://archive.ics.uci.edu/ml; Irvine, CA: University of California, School of Information and Computer Science), or from Kaggle (http://www.kaggle.com/). On some websites, such as the UCI Machine Learning Repository, the datasets are classified by the task you want to perform with the dataset.

Predicted versus Observed Plot

Imagine we have to create a model to predict the price of a house. Click on the **Evaluate** tab:

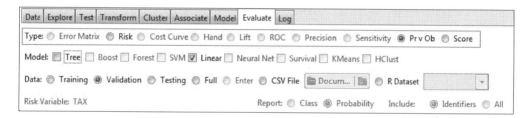

Rattle's **Evaluate** tab offers us two good options for a regression model as shown in the preceding screenshot:

- **Predicted versus Observed Plot**: We will use this option to compare predicted values versus actual values.

- **Score**: As we've seen before, this option creates predictions for the selected dataset:

After creating the model, go to the **Evaluate** tab, select your **Model**, the **Validation** dataset, the **Pr v Ob** option, press **Execute**, and Rattle will build a **Predicted vs. Observed** plot for you, as shown here:

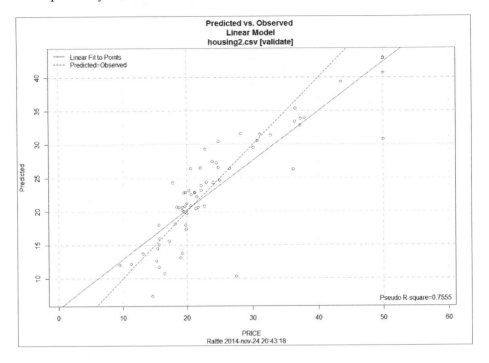

This plot shows a set of points; each point is an observation in the y axes, where we can see the predicted value, and in the x axes, we can see the actual value. We can also see a dotted line; this line represents a perfect prediction, when predicted values are the same as the actual values. The last line is a linear fit to points.

Finally, **Pseudo R-square** is an approach to **R-square**. This measures the variance explained by the model. R-square is a number from 0 to 1; an R-square close to 1 means that the model has strong predictive power. When the model doesn't provide a good prediction, R-square is close to 0. In the same way, a **Pseudo R-square** close to 1 is good; a measure close to 0 means low performance.

Measuring the performance of classifiers

In this section, we'll see how to measure the performance of a classifier. In the example we saw in the previous chapter, a Decision Tree can predict that a new customer will not default, but actually he/she does default. We need a mechanism to evaluate the error rate of a decision tree; this mechanism is the confusion matrix or the error matrix.

Confusion matrix, accuracy, sensitivity, and specificity

Coming back to our loan example, imagine you have classified 1000 loans using a Decision Tree. For each loan, our classifier has added a label with the value *yes* or *no*, depending upon whether the algorithm predicts that the customer will default or not. In order to generalize, we will use the terms positive or negative classification. In our loans example, we have a positive classified observation when our classifier predicted that a customer will default, so the value of the **Default?** Attribute is **Yes**.

In this scenario, there are four types of predictions, listed as follows:

- **True Positive**: The observation has been correctly classified as positive. In our example, the classifier predicts that the customer will default and the customer defaults.

- **False Positive**: The observation has been incorrectly classified as positive. In our example, the classifier predicts that the customer will default but the customer doesn't default.

- **True Negative**: The observation has been correctly classified as negative. In our example, the classifier predicts that the customer will not default and the customer doesn't default.

- **False Negative**: The observation has been incorrectly classified as negative. In our example, the classifier predicts that the customer will not default but the customer defaults.

We will call this classification; the confusion matrix; or the error matrix because we represent it using a matrix, and this, gives us an idea of the prediction error. The following diagram illustrates the confusion matrix:

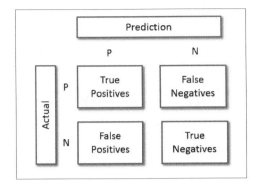

As you can see in the matrix, **True Positives** and **True Negatives** are correctly classified by the algorithm, whereas **False Positives** and **False Negatives** are incorrectly classified. In order to evaluate the performance of the classifier, the first measure is the **accuracy**. To calculate the accuracy, we will divide the total correctly classified observations by all the observations:

$$Accuracy = \frac{Correctly\ classified\ observations}{Total\ Predicted\ observations}$$

The accuracy is a number between 0 and 1. If the accuracy is 0, it means that the classifier has failed in all the predictions; if the accuracy is 1, it means that the classifier has classified correctly, all the observations. When the accuracy is close to one, the performance of the classifier is good, and when the accuracy is close to zero, the performance is bad. If you use a model that randomly guesses whether a credit is classified as bad or good risk (binary classification), the accuracy should be 0.5.

In the following diagram, are the results of two classifiers, **Classifier A** and **Classifier B**, both having 1000 observations, but the **Accuracy** value is very different. In the following example, the performance of **Classifier A** is better than the performance of **Classifier B**:

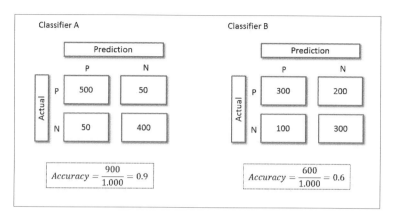

There is no rule for whether an accuracy rate is good or not, because it depends on the problem that you are solving. In order to know if your model has good performance, you have to compare with another model. The first step can be to compare the performance of your model against a random classifier or a simple classifier as baseline. Imagine that by exploring your data, you have discovered that young people have a greater probability of defaulting than older people. You can create a naive classifier that predicts Default?=Yes for young people and Default?=No for older people. If your assumption is true, the accuracy of your naive classifier will be greater than 0.5 (random classifier); maybe 0.6 or 0.7. You can use the performance of this naive model as the baseline to measure the performance of your model.

The opposite measure is the **error rate** — the percentage of observations misclassified.

Accuracy and error rate are good measures towards understanding the performance of a classifier, but keep in mind that they do not distinguish between the types of errors. Imagine you have developed a classifier that classifies tumor images between malignant and benignant. A false positive is a tumor classified as malignant, but that actually benign. If you have a false positive, then probably the doctor will ask for additional tests to confirm the diagnosis, and he will discover that the image was misclassified; but what happens if you have a false negative? If you have a false negative, a malignant tumor will be classified as benign. Probably, the doctor won't ask for additional tests and a malignant tumor would be treated as a benign tumor.

As you can see, for this domain, a false negative is more dangerous than a false positive. For this reason, we need a way to differentiate between the kinds of misclassifications.

We can use the **Sensitivity** or **True Positive Rate** to measure the ability of a classifier to correctly classify positive observations:

$$Sensitivity = \frac{True\ Positive}{Positive} = \frac{True\ Positive}{True\ Positive + False\ Negative}$$

If a classifier has a high sensitivity, this means that when an observation is classified as positive, the probability of error is low.

In order to measure the ability of a classifier to correctly classify a negative case, we will use **Specificity** or **True Negative Rate**:

$$Sensitivity = \frac{True\ Negative}{Negative} = \frac{True\ Negative}{True\ Negative + False\ Negative}$$

Now, we'll use the model that we built in the previous chapter to explore Rattle's confusion matrix options, to classify the risk of loan applications into two classes: 1 (good credit risk) and 2 (bad credit risk). Load the dataset we used in *Chapter 6, Decision Trees and Other Supervised Learning Methods*, and create two different models. I've created a decision tree (Minimum Split = 30, Minimum Bucket = 20, and Maximum Depth = 10) and a Random Forest model (default parameters).

Now, go to Rattle's **Evaluate** tab. You have three rows of options. In the top row (highlighted in the following screenshot), you can choose the type of evaluation you want to perform. Choose **Error Matrix** (confusion matrix). The middle row is for the model you want to evaluate. As explained earlier, I've created two models, a decision tree and a random forest, so I have the option of calculating the confusion matrix for these models. In the following screenshot, you can see that I've selected **Tree** and **Forest** because I want to compare the confusion matrix of both the models.

Finally, the bottom row allows you to choose the dataset that we'll use to perform the evaluation. By default, Rattle chooses the **Validation** dataset. Usually, we use this dataset to optimize the model, as shown in this screenshot:

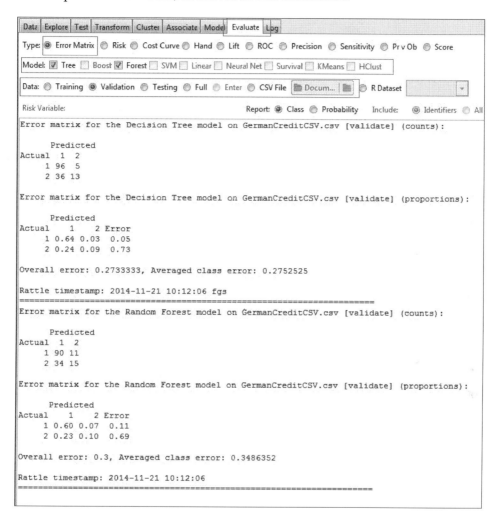

In the previous screenshot, we can see the output of the **Error Matrix** option. For each model, we can see the confusion matrix with the total number of observations and the percentage of observations. After the matrix, Rattle provides us with the error rate or **Overall error**.

Risk Chart

For binary classification models, Risk Chart, or Cumulative Gain Chart, is a good way to measure model performance.

To obtain a Risk Chart, after creating a binary classification model, go to the **Evaluate** tab, choose the **Risk** type and the **Validation** dataset, and press **Execute**, as shown here:

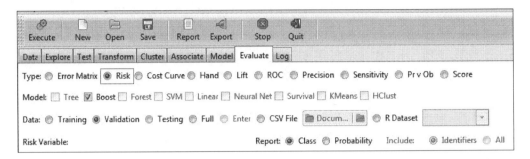

In the following screenshot, we can see a Risk Chart for our credit example. In this example, we've 1000 credit applications, 700 classified as a good risk and 300 classified as bad risk. We have a risk score of 33 percent. The risk of giving credit to an application classified as bad risk is 33 percent.

Imagine we want to use our model to choose some applications to inspect before granting a credit. We would like that our model helps us to choose the most risky applications. The Risk Chart will explain whether our model is appropriate for that task. The following screenshot demonstrates this:

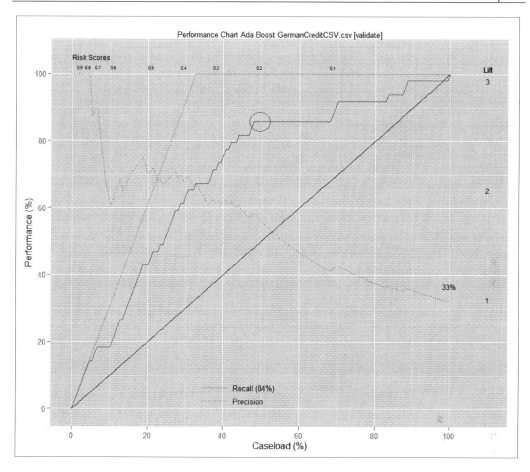

In order to understand a Risk Chart, we need to know two important concepts—
Precision and **Recall**. In a classification problem, precision is the percentage of
positive observations that are correctly classified by the model:

$$Precision = \frac{True\ Positive}{True\ Positive - False\ Positive}$$

A model with a high recall will be able to find the positive observations in our dataset; Recall and Sensitivity are the same. The formula is shown here:

$$Recall = Sensitivity = \frac{True\,Positive}{Positive} = \frac{True\,Positive}{True\,Positive - False\,Negative}$$

In the y axes, we can see the percentage of positive observations or **Performance (%)** applications classified as bad risk.

In the x axes, we can see the percentage of observations or **Caseload (%)**: 1000 credit applications.

In this plot, the diagonal line is a baseline, if we review credit applications randomly. To review 50 percent of bad risk applications, we need to review 50 percent of applications.

The **Recall** line shows us how the model ranks the applications. If we review 500 applications selected by the model (50 percent of the whole dataset), we'll review approximately 84 percent of the bad risk applications.

ROC Curve

The ROC Curve is a chart that shows the performance of a binary classification model. This chart plots **True Positive Rate** (sensitivity) versus the **False Positive Rate** of our model.

Imagine that we want to develop a binary classification model to classify new loan applications into high risk applications and low risk applications. We have a model that returns the probability of fraud. We need to choose a threshold to split applications between low and high risk. For example, if the probability of fraud is higher or equal than 0.7 we predict *high risk*, and *low risk* if the probability is lower than 0.7. We can try with different thresholds and we'll discover that with higher thresholds, we obtain lower true positive rates and higher false positives rates, and with lower thresholds, we will obtain higher true positive rates and lower false positive rates. Obviously, there is a trade-off between true positive rate and false positive rate; the ROC Curve represents this trade-off for our model and helps us understand the model performance.

A good way to measure the accuracy of a classifier is the Area Under the ROC Curve or **AUC**. An area of 1 represents a perfect classifier; an area of 0.5 represents a random classifier. The ROC Curve of our model will be a number between 0 and 1. A rule of thumb to understand the **AUC** is:

- 1 to 0.90: Excellent
- 0.90 to 0.80: Good
- 0.70 to 0.80: Correct
- 0.70 to 0.60: Poor
- 0.60 to 0.50: Bad

In the following screenshot, you can see the ROC Curve of our credit risk example. The diagonal line is the ROC Curve for a random classifier, and we can use it as a baseline to compare the performance of our model. As you can see in the screenshot, the area under the baseline curve is 0.5. In the screenshot, you can see that the Area Under the Curve or **AUC** is 0.8:

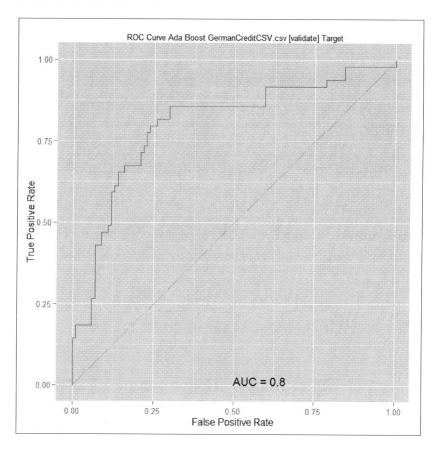

Further learning

In the previous chapter, I recommended that you pursue *Introduction to Data Science*, a Coursera course by Bill Howe, Director of Research Scalable Data Analytics at the University of Washington. The seventh lecture of this course has two interesting videos on Overfitting, Evaluation, and Cross-validation. This is an introductory course and the videos are very intuitive.

Also, a very nice introductory book is *Data Science for Business* written by Foster Provost and Tom Fawcett, *O'Reilly Media*. This is a great book for a manager who needs to understand data science. The book has a nice chapter about overfitting and model evaluation.

Summary

In this chapter, we saw different ways of analyzing the performance of supervised models. We started with regression model evaluation and then we moved on to classification models performance.

For regression models, we saw that the difference between predicted values and actual values is the most important measure. In this way, Rattle provides the Predicted versus Observed Plot.

We discovered that in classification, a false positive is different from a false negative. Based on this difference, we can create a confusion matrix and evaluate the performance of a classifier using different mechanisms such as a Risk Chart, or ROC Curve.

In this chapter, we've worked with Rattle because it provides the necessary tools to evaluate the performance of a model developed with it. In the next chapter, we'll come back to Qlik Sense to learn the key concepts of data visualization and learn how to communicate with data.

8
Visualizations, Data Applications, Dashboards, and Data Storytelling

In this chapter, we'll focus on data visualization. Representing your data and insights visually will help business users to understand it. A good data application allows the business user to explore data, understand it, and discover new things.

Usually, a dashboard is a visual representation of the most important **Key Performance Indicator (KPI)** of a company, department, or business process. A dashboard can be created on a sheet of paper, in a spreadsheet, or with the help of a data visualization tool such as Qlik Sense.

When you create a dashboard with Qlik Sense, you create a live application. A Qlik Sense application can take the form of a dashboard or an analytic application. As you will see in this chapter, Qlik Sense allows you to combine this dashboard, analysis, and reporting in the same data application.

In data visualizations; charts, tables and other visualizations are the building blocks. We'll start by describing the visualizations provided by Qlik Sense and look at some basic rules to create them. We're not going to explain how to create a chart in Qlik Sense, because we did that in *Chapter 4, Creating Your First Qlik Sense Application*.

After data visualization, we'll discuss how to create a data application. We'll focus on the important features of Qlik Sense and on one particular approach to data application design.

Finally, we'll focus on data storytelling, a way to present your data and conclusions.

Data visualization in Qlik Sense

In *Chapter 4, Creating Your First Qlik Sense Application*, we saw how to create a Qlik Sense application. We also saw how to load data and how to create charts. The objective of this chapter is not to create a lot of charts. We are going to explore, in detail, a bar chart to explore the configuration options and we'll describe the charts provided by Qlik Sense and when to use the different data visualizations. We'll also look at some ideas on how to create data visualizations.

Visualization toolbox

To see all the available options, open a Qlik Sense application in **Edit** mode and you will find all the options in the left hand pane. In the following screenshot, we can see the **Charts pane**:

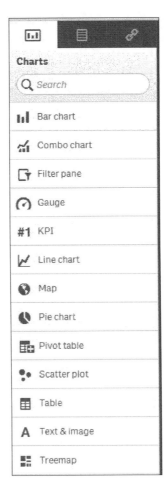

Qlik Sense provides the following default charts:

- **Bar chart**: This is the simplest chart, it helps us to answer questions such as "Who are my best customers?" and "Who are the top performing salespeople?".

- **Combo chart**: In this chart, you can combine bars, lines, and points or symbols. I like to use it to represent metrics of different types such as sales and margins; you can use bars to represent the amount of sales and points to represent the margin.

- **Filter pane**: You can use a filter pane to contain the most common filters such as the year, month, or country; in this way, the user has easy access to the most common filters.

- **Gauge** and **KPI**: These charts only represents a metric with no dimensions. The Gauge chart shows the metric like a speedometer (**Radial Gauge**) or like a thermometer (**Bar Gauge**) and the KPI chart shows the metric as a text. Be careful when representing a single metric; if a dashboard tells us that the amount of sales is € **318,000**, we don't know if the performance is high or low. If you compare the amount of sales with another metric like the target or the last year sales, this will add context to our metric. In the following screenshot you can see the same metric as a Radial Gauge, Bar Gauge, and KPI.

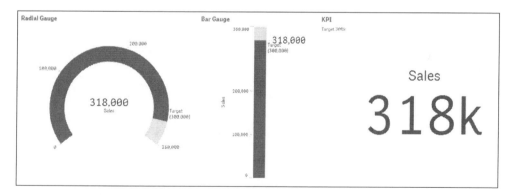

- **Line chart**: This chart is very useful when showing the evolution of a metric over time.

- **Map**: A different way to discover patterns in data is to visualize data in a map. By adding a location to your business data, you are providing a new context that can help you to obtain new insights. In Qlik Sense, there are two types of map polygons or area maps, as well as slippy maps or point maps.

- **Pie chart**: Sometimes, we need to see how a metric such as sales is distributed; the pie chart is a very effective method to show distributions. Be careful, if our dimension has a lot of values, this chart can get confusing.

- **Scatter plot**: To discover if two quantitative values are correlated and to which degree, we can use a scatter plot. With a scatter plot, we can see if there is a correlation between two variables.

- **Table** and **Pivot Table**: Tables are very useful when studying exact numbers or details.

- **Text & image**: By using text and image objects we can combine text, images, and measures. This is very useful in the main sheet of a dashboard. Usually, you place the headlines in this first sheet, and you can use the font size and type to provide more relevance to a text or value.

- **Treemap**: A treemap is a very useful tool to represent hierarchical (tree-structured) data. In a treemap, each branch is plotted as a rectangle, split by other branches or leaves. Finally, each leaf is plotted as a rectangle, the size of this rectangle depends on the measure's value. In the following screenshot, **Europe** and **America** are two branches and the countries are leaves:

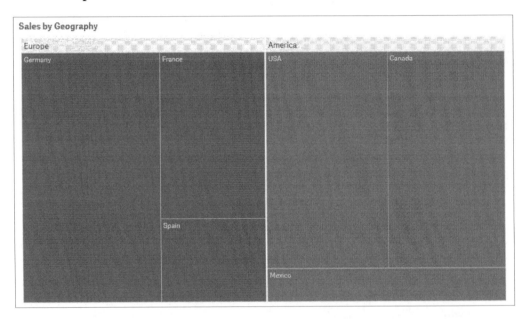

- **Extensions**: Qlik Sense allows developers to create *Extensions*, which are additional developments that extend Qlik Sense functionality. There are several websites where you can find extensions, such as the following:

  - **Qlik Community** (http://community.qlik.com/): This is a very active community about Qlik Sense and Qlik View.

- ○ **Qlik Market** (`http://market.qlik.com/`): This is an exchange platform for useful solutions. There are three types of solutions: **Connectors**, **Applications**, and **Extensions**. This site is a very useful resource. Some extensions are free and some of them are chargeable.

- ○ **Qlik Branch** (`http://branch.qlik.com/`): This is a collaborative site for developers to share their projects and extensions. You can find extensions and other developments that add functionalities to Qlik Sense.

You can find detailed instructions on how to use each chart on YouTube. Qlik has a channel called **Qlik** and there is a very good series called **Qlik Sense Desktop Tutorials**.

Qlik Sense charts are Responsible and Smart. The charts adapt themselves to the space to show information to the user in the smartest possible way. These kinds of charts are very useful for mobile devices. We're using Qlik Desktop, which is a PC based tool but, when using Qlik Sense Enterprise, we can access and develop from a PC, tablet, or smartphone and the Smart Charts adapt to the available space. The ability of the charts to adapt to space is very important for mobility purposes. If we access Qlik Sense with a browser from any device, from a cell phone to a desktop, every component in Qlik Sense is able to adapt to the available display screen space.

Creating a bar chart

A good visualization or chart has to be *clear*, *complete*, and *necessary*. The user needs to be able to understand the visualization, for this reason you have to remember the following:

- Avoid complex charts
- Include legends whenever necessary
- Label axes
- Include titles, subtitles, and footnotes wherever necessary

Each visualization is a message and it's important that each chart has a complete meaning of its own. Finally, use only the necessary chart to avoid hiding the important ones in an ocean of plots.

In this section, we will use a simple bar chart to explore most of the configuration options of a Qlik Sense chart. In a bar chart, you have different values side-by-side. This chart is very useful when looking at the difference between dimensions. You can look over your sales in the different regions and it is very easy to compare actual versus planned, or see the differences between regions. You can use this chart for rank analysis or to show the top values, like the best sales representatives or the bestselling products.

To create a bar chart, I've created a small dataset with the final classification of Liga BBVA 2014-2015, the Spanish soccer league, as shown in the following screenshot:

Rank	Team	Points	Played	Won	Drawn	Lost	Golas For	Goals Against
1	FC Barcelona	94	38	30	4	4	110	21
2	Real Madrid	92	38	30	2	6	118	38
3	Atlético Madrid	78	38	23	9	6	67	29
4	Valencia CF	77	38	22	11	5	70	32
5	Sevilla FC	76	38	23	7	8	71	45
6	Villarreal CF	60	38	16	12	10	48	37
7	Athletic Club	55	38	15	10	13	42	41
8	RC Celta	51	38	13	12	13	47	44
9	Málaga CF	50	38	14	8	16	42	48
10	RCD Espanyol	49	38	13	10	15	47	51
11	Rayo Vallecano	49	38	15	4	19	46	68
12	Real Sociedad	46	38	11	13	14	44	51
13	Elche CF	41	38	11	8	19	35	62
14	Levante UD	37	38	9	10	19	34	67
15	Getafe CF	37	38	10	7	21	33	64
16	RC Deportivo	35	38	7	14	17	35	60
17	Granada CF	35	38	7	14	17	29	64
18	SD Eibar	35	38	9	8	21	34	55
19	UD Almería	32	38	8	8	22	35	64
20	Córdoba CF	20	38	3	11	24	22	68

Our objective is to create a chart like the following:

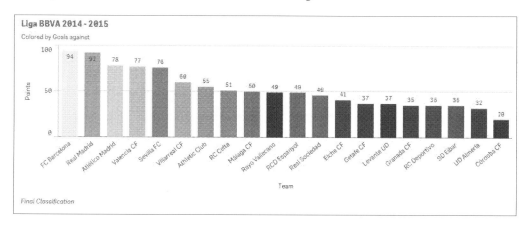

This chart shows us the final classification, the number of points for each team and we used color to represent *goals against*. The chart tells us that FC Barcelona won the league and Real Madrid was second. Real Madrid and FC Barcelona were very close because the final number of points are very similar. In general, the teams with more goals against, perform worse; for this reason the bars on the right are darker than the bars on the left. There are two exceptions: Real Madrid and Rayo Vallecano. Real Madrid have more goals against than Atlético de Madrid or Valencia but have a better placing; probably they scored a lot of goals. Rayo Vallecano have the same issue as Real Madrid; they have a lot of goals against. As you can see, bar charts are very simple but they can provide a lot of information.

From the previous chapters, you know how to load data and how to create a bar chart. In this chart, we used **Team** for the dimension and **Points** for the measure.

To personalize bar charts, we've four main menus:

- **Data**
- **Sorting**
- **Add-ons**
- **Appearance**

These menus are illustrated in the following screenshot:

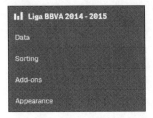

In this section, we're going to describe these four menus; they are similar in all charts.

The Data menu

To create a chart to represent the final placing at the end of the season, the first important decision is what to represent in the chart. The dimension is very obvious, we choose the variable **Team**. For measure, there are different options, such as **Rank**, or **Points**. If we use **Rank** as the measure, we'll see the final rank, but if we use **Points**, we'll see the final rank and the difference in points between teams. In this example, we've used **Points** because it provides us with more information:

From the previous chapters, you already know how to set **Points** and **Team** as the measure and dimension. In this example, we're going to focus on a few additional settings that will help us customize the chart.

In the **Dimensions** box, we see two interesting options, as follows:

- The **Show null values** checkbox
- The **Limitation** checklist

The **Show null values** checkbox tells us what to do when the value of the dimension is null. In the following piece from the original dataset, we've deleted the name of a football team; if the checkbox is checked, Qlik Sense will place a - in the place of the team name. If the checkbox is unchecked, Qlik Sense will draw RC Celta and RCD Espanyol, and will omit the ninth team, as illustrated here:

8	RC Celta	51	38	13	12	13	47	44
9		50	38	14	8	16	42	48
10	RCD Espanyol	49	38	13	10	15	47	51

This check is very useful when looking for problems in your dataset. Imagine that you have a dataset with sales transactions; each row contains product, amount sold, customer, and salesman. If you plot a chart with amount sold as the measure and Product, Customer or Salesman as the dimension, a value of amount sold with - as label, this means that, in the original dataset, one or more rows have missing values for the dimension; as happened with the ninth team in our previous example.

The second important setting in dimensions is the **Limitation** listbox. This setting limits the number of values that Qlik Sense plots. There are four possible options, as depicted in the following table:

Limitation	Illustration	Description
No limitation	Limitation **No limitation** ▼	Qlik Sense will plot all possible dimensions; in our example Qlik Sense will plot all teams.
Fixed number	Limitation **Fixed number** ▼ **Top** Bottom 10 *fx* Calculated on measure: Points	Qlik Sense will plot a fixed number of values (teams). This option is useful to create a Top 10 analysis.

Limitation	Illustration	Description
Exact value	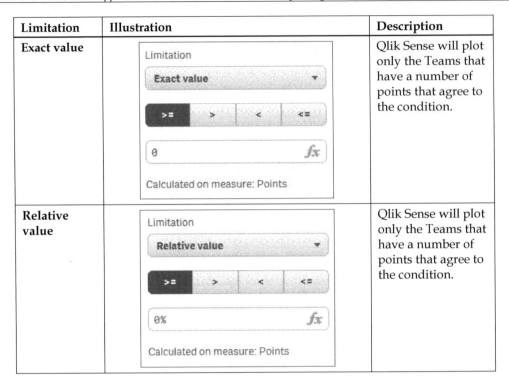	Qlik Sense will plot only the Teams that have a number of points that agree to the condition.
Relative value		Qlik Sense will plot only the Teams that have a number of points that agree to the condition.

An important setting for the measure is **Number formatting**. By default, this setting option is **Auto**; generally Qlik Sense selects the best option, but if you want to be sure how the numbers are going to be formatted, you can set it however you wish. An example setting is shown here:

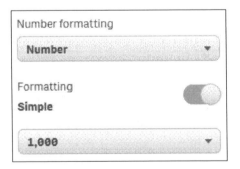

You can choose between these different **Number formatting** settings:

- **Auto**
- **Number**
- **Money**
- **Date**
- **Duration**
- **Custom**

For **Money**, **Date** and **Duration**, Qlik Sense Desktop takes the format from the first lines in **Load Script**. Qlik Sense Desktop automatically creates these lines from your computer's local settings. You can use the **Custom** option to create your own formatting mask.

The Sorting menu

The **Sorting** menu allows us to personalize how values are sorted in our bar chart. This menu looks like this:

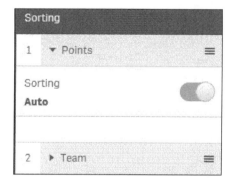

In this example, we can sort the values by the measure, **Points,** or by the dimension, **Team**. Qlik Sense Desktop chooses the top variable to sort the values; in this case we will use **Points** to sort the values. If two teams have the same amount of points, they will be sorted by the second variable; in this case, **Team**.

If we place **Team** at the top of the variable list, the values will be sorted alphabetically by the name of the team.

As you can see in the previous screenshot, Qlik Sense Desktop sets the sorting type, by default, to **Auto**. You can set this option to **Custom** and personalize how you want to sort the values.

The Add-ons menu

This menu provides us with the personalization options, **Data handling** and **Reference lines**, as shown in this screenshot:

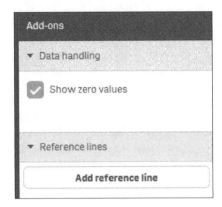

Data Handling has only one option: **Show zero values**. If this option is checked, as shown in the preceding screenshot, Qlik Sense Desktop plots a team with zero points. If we uncheck this option, Qlik Sense Desktop does not plot a team with zero points.

With **Reference lines** we can add horizontal lines to our bar chart. In the following screenshot, you can see how to set a line by taking the points average:

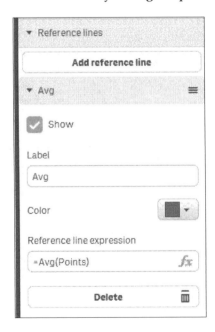

The Appearance menu

The **Appearance** menu has five options, as listed here:

- **General**
- **Presentation**
- **Colors and legend**
- **X-axis**
- **Y-axis**

This menu is illustrated in the following screenshot:

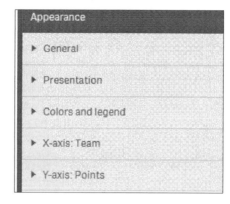

Under the **General** submenu, there are the **Title**, **Subtitle**, and **Footnote** options. When you see an **fx** symbol in the textbox, it means that you can use an expression. We're going to use this functionality in the following example.

In the **Presentation** submenu, we can choose between **Vertical** and **Horizontal** orientation, the type of grid, and whether we use the **Value labels** switch, to plot the value of each bar in the bar chart. In this example, if you turn on this switch, the amount of points for each team will be plotted in each bar.

The **X-axis** and **Y-axis** submenus allow us to personalize labels and titles for each axis. If the variable is numeric, such as **Points**, we can also personalize the axis range.

The **Appearance** menu is further illustrated as follows:

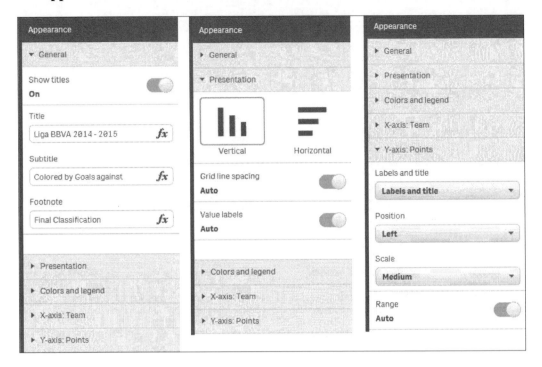

Finally, using the **Colors and legend** submenu, we can personalize the color of each bar. Qlik Sense Desktop offers us four options:

- **Single color**: All bars have the same color.
- **By dimension**: Each different value in the dimension variable has a different color. In our example, each team has a different color. We used this option in *Chapter 4, Creating Your First Qlik Sense Application*.

- **By measure**: In our example, Qlik Sense Desktop uses the variable **Points** to color each bar.

- **By expression**: In this option, we can use a new expression to color the bars. This option is very useful because it allows us to code more information in the same plot. In this example we used the variable **Goals Against**; in this way we discovered that Real Madrid and Rayo Vallecano conceded an unusual number of goals. The expression can return a number, as in this example, or a color code, as in the example in *Chapter 5, Clustering and Other Unsupervised Learning Methods*.

In the next section, we're going to use title and subtitle expressions to add information to our chart.

Data analysis, data applications, and dashboards

Before creating a data application, you have to define who is going to use your application and what the objective of the application is. Patricia L. Saporito, in *Applied Insurance Analytics, Pearson Education LTD* defines three main user groups:

- **Executive management**: They need key metrics, very visual applications and should be able to access the analysis from different devices

- **Middle managers**: They need key metrics and the ability to navigate from aggregate data to detailed data

- **Analysts**: This group needs to be able to manipulate data on the lowest grain and create new metrics

You also need to be familiar with the metrics you are going to use in your application. A special type of metric is a **Key Performance Indicator** (**KPI**). KPIs explain the performance of a business process or activity; Sales versus Objective would be a good KPI for a **Sales Performance** dashboard. As you can see, KPIs are metrics that illustrate performance but, to understand the reasons of this performance, we need intermediate metrics; Opportunity Win Rate would be a good metric to help us to understand the Sales versus Objective metric.

In this section, we'll discuss how to structure data applications with Qlik Sense Desktop. We'll start by describing the important data analysis characteristics of Qlik Sense Desktop. Then we'll focus on how to structure a Qlik Sense Desktop application.

Qlik Sense data analysis

Qlik Sense and QlikView are different tools. QlikView is a great tool for developing guided analytic applications, and Qlik Sense is a tool for self-service visualization and data analysis, but QlikView and Qlik Sense share the same principles in their analytic engine. Qlik Sense is a new tool but its analytic engine is the new version of the successful QlikView engine. In this section, we'll review the most important characteristics of this engine and how these characteristics influence our analysis.

In-memory analysis

Traditional **Business Intelligence (BI)** or data analysis tools access the data through a database. Databases are based on filesystems, and data access in a filesystem is not fast. For this reason, traditional BI doesn't provide a great interactive experience. When a user makes a selection, the BI tool executes a query to the database, the database then needs to access a lot of rows, sometimes millions of rows in the filesystem and aggregate them to provide the result; this entire process is time consuming and the user has to wait for the information. The result is that the user perceives a lack of interactivity and doesn't use the tool. To avoid this, BI tools aggregate data to reduce the number of rows. For example, in a sales analysis application, the raw data is sales tickets; each row in the dataset is a line ticket. If you aggregate the sales information by store and day, you have the amount of sales in a week for a given store. You have reduced the number of rows and you will improve your response time, but you have lost information and your analysis will be limited.

In order to provide a good level of interactivity and avoid aggregating data, Qlik Sense works in a different way to the traditional BI. When you open a Qlik Sense application, the engine loads all the data for you to the RAM. This memory is very fast and Qlik offers great performance without aggregating data. Thanks to its *in-memory* approach, Qlik Sense is a very interactive tool and we can take advantage of the most detailed atomic data. Keeping the most atomic data in our dataset allows us to develop our data application using a **Dashboard Analysis and Reporting (DAR)** approach.

Qlik introduced in-memory analysis in 1993. Today, other vendors are developing in-memory tools to analyze data. In my opinion, the QIX Associative Data Indexing Engine makes best use of these decades of experience.

Associative experience

In a traditional database data model, different tables are linked together with pre-declared keys and the user only can explore his/her data through predefined paths.

The Qlik Sense engine uses a different approach. In Qlik's engine, all data is associated, and the user can consult the analytic engine without any predefined paths. After installing Qlik Sense, you have three example applications. We're going to use an example application to understand the magic of associative logic. Open Qlik Sense, open the **Sales Discovery** app, and open the Data model.

The data model is organized around a table called **SalesDetails** that contains the most atomic data of a sale—price, quantity, discount, product, customer, and so on. This table contains the field we want to measure and we call it the **fact table**:

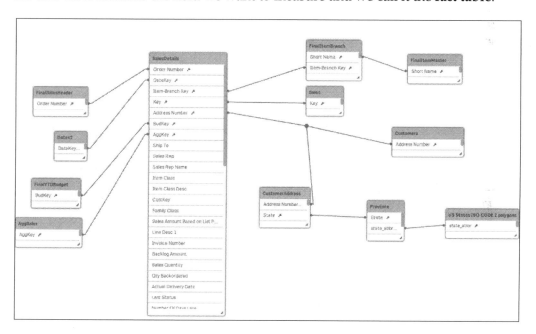

Our objective is to obtain Californian customers who bought Alcoholic Beverages in January 2014. Go to **App overview** and open any sheet in the application. In the top right square, click the squared icon to open a filter screen, marked by the red arrow in the following screenshot:

As you can see in the following screenshot, we use the search box to look for a filter. Enter **Year** in the search box; Qlik Sense will give you the **Year** filter, select **2014**. Repeat this for **Alcoholic Beverages**, **CA**, and **Jan**. Finally, enter **customer** in the search box to obtain the **Customer** filter; in this filter, you see a white list of customers. These customers are associated with **Jan**, **2014**, **CA**, **Alcoholic Beverage**; this means that these customers have bought **Alcoholic Beverages** in California. After this white list, there is a grey list of customers. These customers are not associated with my selections; this means that these customers have not bought **Alcoholic Beverages** in January **2014** or they are not from California:

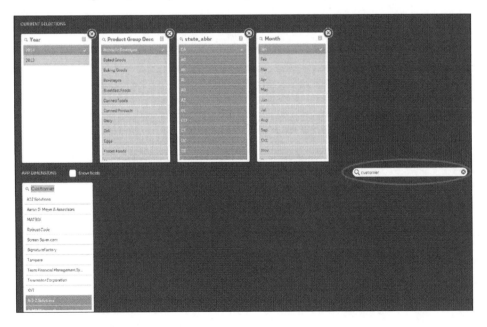

Thanks to the associative logic, a business user can freely explore his/her information and obtain answers to his questions. Now try posing and answering your own questions.

A lot of people has written articles about the Associative Experience, I especially like the one written by *Michael Tarallo*, *The Associative Experience - Revisited*: `https://community.qlik.com/blogs/theqlikviewblog/2014/04/10/the-associative-experience--revisited`

Data applications and dashboards

There are different approaches to designing data applications. As we've seen, the design of the application is defined by the audience, the business objective, and the data, but a very popular approach in QlikView and Qlik Sense is **DAR**.

The DAR approach

DAR stands for **Dashboard, Analysis and Reporting** and is a very useful approach proposed by Qlik to develop data analysis applications in Qlik Sense. We'll use the **Sales Discovery** app to explain this concept.

In a DAR application, the first sheet offers us the headlines of our application. This part of the application is the dashboard. In the following screenshot, you can see the **Performance Dashboard** sheet from the **Sales Discovery** application:

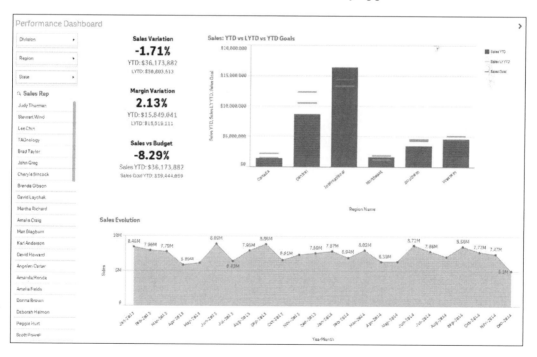

In the central area, we can see that, during 2014, the company sold **1.71**% less than in the same period of 2013, the margin was **2.13**%, and sales were **8.29**% below target. We can also see a bar chart that explains how the different regions are performing. This sheet is designed to explain performance and where we have to focus our attention. Just by looking at this sheet, we can see that sales performance is very low and that the **Central** region is the one with the worst performance.

In the dashboard we focus only on a few KPI, as in the headlines in a newspaper. Users will use this sheet to discover a performance gap, and then they'll move to the analysis part. In the same initial sheet, select the **Central** region and the sheet will become the **Performance Dashboard** for the **Central** region. Now you can see that sales are **30.07**% below budget and the following bar chart shows the performance of the states in the **Central** region. This chart tells us that we should focus on Minnesota (**MN**) so select **MN** in the bar chart:

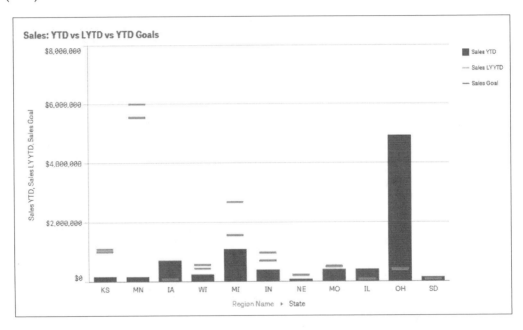

Now, to continue analyzing this low performance in Minnesota, go to the **Top Customers** sheet. You've moved to a different sheet but Qlik Sense keeps your current selection. You are in the **Top Customers** sheet, analyzing data from **Central Region** and Minnesota. In the top bar of the screen, you can see the filters, as shown in this screenshot:

The **Top Customers** bar chart shows the best customers from 2013 and 2014. Now select the year **2013** and then the year **2014** and compare the Top Customers. You can see that the difference in sales between **2013** and **2014** is that **Paracel** and **Renegade info Crew** were the best customers in 2013, but in 2014 they bought less, as depicted in the following screenshot:

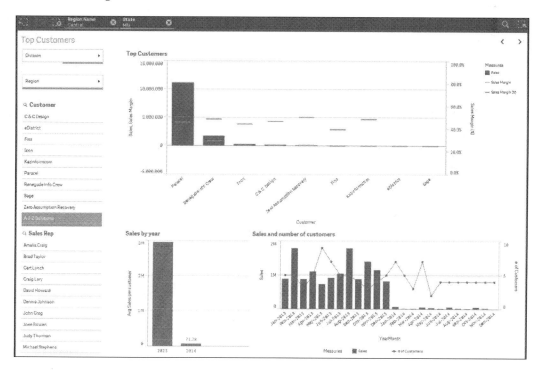

We started looking at sales deviation in our dashboard. Then, in the analysis phase, we discovered the reasons for this deviation.

Finally, we're going to enter into the reporting phase where we'll obtain the most granular information that is responsible for the deviation.

In this case, I would like to find out the details of purchases of these customers. Select these customers and go to the **Transactions** sheet. At the top of the screenshot, you can see that we've selected the **Central** region, the **MN** state, **Paracel**, and **Renegade info Crew**. In the following screenshot, you can see the table of all transactions in Minnesota by these customers:

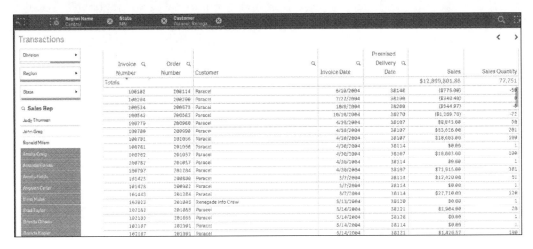

As we've seen, we started at the dashboard level where we saw low performance. Then we analyzed this deviation and, finally, we reported the details or the reasons for this deviation.

Data storytelling with Qlik Sense

Generally, when you present your conclusion to a group of executives, your presentation competes for their time and attention with a lot of different things. Using your data to explain a story is powerful because stories have the following characteristics:

- Memorable
- Impactful
- Personal

Using storytelling to present your data or insights can help you to do the following:

- Keep the interest of your audience
- Explain complex concepts
- Convince people
- Make your presentation memorable

There is a lot of good literature around storytelling and data storytelling. The objective of this section is just present this Qlik Sense functionality but I would like to share my trick to prepare presentations. Usually, in our daily work, we need to prepare a presentation within a limited preparation time. Personally, I use a notepad (not a digital one) and I write down my outline in seven fundamental building blocks:

- **Audience**: Everything starts with the audience. A presentation for IT is very different from a presentation for a business unit. Ask yourself, what are the concerns of your audience? Why are they interested in your story?

- **Objective**: What is your objective? Do you want your audience to make a decision? Is it just an informative presentation? Having your objective in mind is really important when creating your story.

- **Key messages**: Time and attention are very limited; writing down your key messages will help you to focus your story.

- **The story**: Draw your story and choose the data visualization you are going to use. Choose the visualizations that help you to explain your story. Are they relevant? Take time restrictions into consideration.

- **The link between the slides or between visualizations**: Links between slides are sentences that avoid breaking the flow of the story between slides. Different slides in a story can break the flow of the story and make your presentation just a collection of slides. For this reason, I prepare every link between two slides.

- **Review everything**: After we have noted down the preceding building blocks, we have to ask ourselves the following questions:

  - Are the key messages clearly explained in the story?
  - Are you focusing only on key messages?
  - Do the visualizations support the story?
  - Are the visualizations clear?
  - Does the story support the objective and the key messages?
  - Is your story and its content suitable for your audience?

Qlik Sense Desktop has a great tool for data storytelling. To open a data story, click the **Stories** button and choose the **Shipment delays impact** story, as shown in this screenshot:

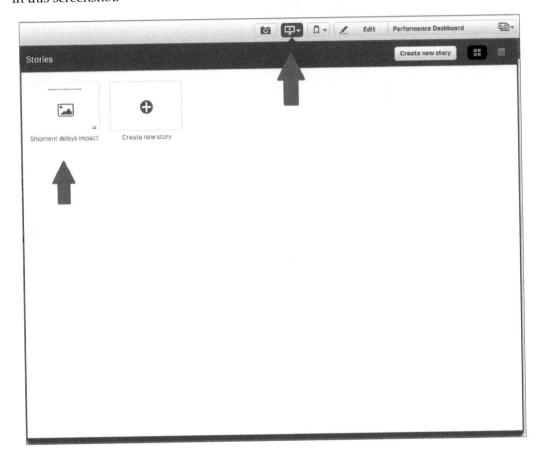

As you can see in the following screenshot, press the **Play** button to start the story:

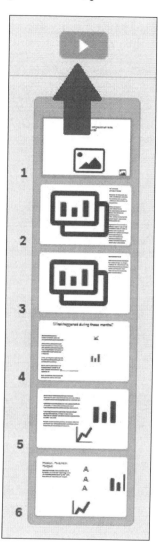

The presentation mode has arrow buttons at the right and at the left, to go forward or backward in your presentation. When you present your insights, people will have questions about the data; by pressing the **Go to sheet** button, you can open the data application and show them the data, as illustrated in this screenshot:

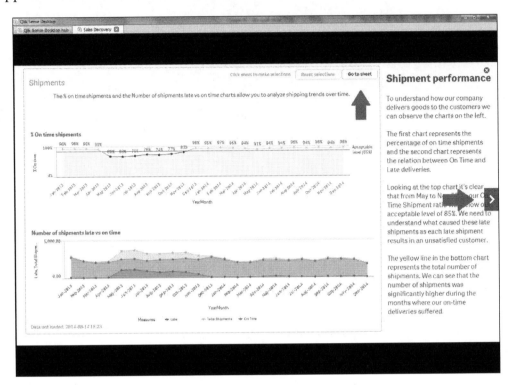

Creating a new story

To create a new story, you need to take some snapshots of your data visualizations. Go to the application, open a sheet, and press the camera button, marked by the arrow:

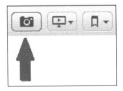

Now the charts are in snapshot mode and the visualizations are highlighted with a dotted line; you just need to click on the chart and Qlik Sense will take a snapshot that you will be able to use to create a story, as shown here:

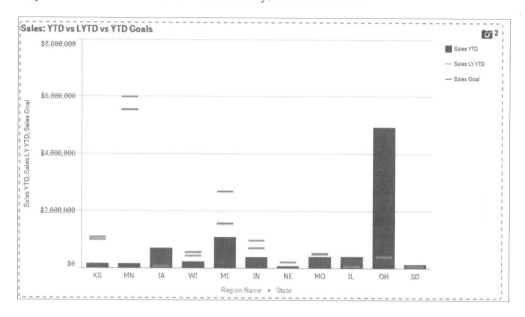

Finally, we have some data snapshots we can use to create a new story. We have to go to the top area of the screen, press the **stories** button, and press the **Create new story** button:

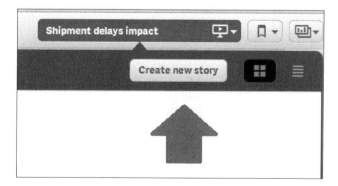

Choose a name for the story and start creating it. To create your story, you have five main components:

- **Camera Tool**: Using this tool, you can capture the charts
- **Text**: Using this tool, you can add titles or paragraphs
- **Shapes**: Use this tool, to point to any data
- **Effects**: You can use this tool to add effects to the charts to highlight special data
- **Images**: Using this tool, add images from the media library

The following screenshot shows the five components:

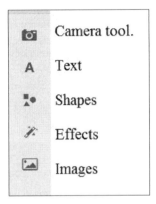

Now you can create a sheet using these components just by dragging and dropping the components into the sheet.

We've added a blank slide and we've added charts, effects, text, and images but we can also add live slides by embedding a sheet into a slide. In the bottom left area, click the plus sign to add a new slide. There are three types of slides:

- **Blank**: This is a slide like the one we've just created
- **Sheet left-aligned**: This is a slide with a left aligned embedded sheet
- **Sheet**: This is a slide with an embedded sheet

These slides are illustrated in the following screenshot:

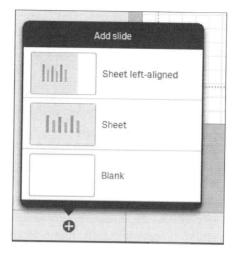

Select **Sheet left-aligned** or **Sheet** and choose a sheet for your slide. You will get a blank sheet into which you can drag and drop components, as well as customizing them according to your preference. The following screenshot shows a **360 Analysis** sheet that has been customized:

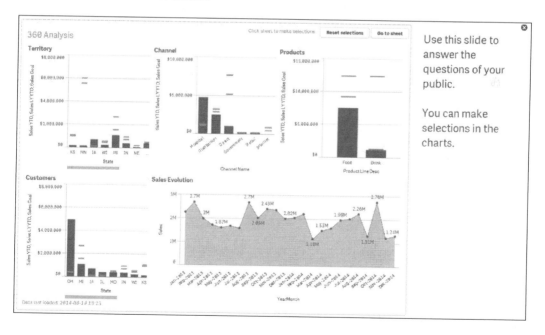

The **Go to Sheet** button and the inclusion of a live sheet in a slide give the opportunity to bring your story to life and handle audience questions.

Further learning

We've introduced data visualization. If you are interested in improving your knowledge of this huge topic, Stephen Few and Edward R. Tufte are probably the best authors to consult. Some great books on this topic are:

- *Learning QlikView Data Visualization* by Karl Pover, *PACKT Publishing*. This is a QlikView book but I had a great time with it and the principles are still valid.

- *Information Dashboard Design, Displaying data for at-a-glance monitoring, Stephen Few, Analytics Press.*

- *Visualize this The FlowingData Guide to Design, Visualization and Statistics, by Nathan Yau, Wiley Publishing, Inc.*

We've seen the **DAR** approach or **Dashboard**, **Analysis** and **Reporting** relating to the design of data applications.

To gain a deeper understanding of the DAR methodology, have a look at a technical paper on the Qlik Design Blog:

```
https://community.qlik.com/blogs/qlikviewdesignblog/2013/11/08/dar-
methodology
```

Finally, related to data storytelling, I found this book helpful:

Strategic Storytelling, How to Create Persuasive Business Presentations, by Dave McKinsey, *CreateSpace Independent Publishing Platform.*

Summary

In this chapter, we've focused on Qlik Sense and how to communicate insights and the analyses you've made.

We started with data visualization; we created a bar chart and discussed other charts.

After data visualization, we discussed Qlik Sense functionalities which make it a great tool, not just for data visualization, but also for data analysis. These characteristics are the in-memory engine, the associative logic, and the fact that Qlik Sense doesn't need to pre-aggregate data; in Qlik Sense, you can load atomic data in memory and you can aggregate at runtime.

We've also seen the **DAR** approach or **Dashboard, Analysis and Reporting** in the design of data applications.

Finally, we defined data storytelling and reviewed Qlik Sense data storytelling capabilities.

In the next chapter, we'll create a data application. We'll start by defining the planning of the application, exploring the data, creating our predictions with Rattle, and finally, we'll create a data application using Qlik Sense.

Developing a Complete Application

9

A business needs to forecast demand in order to plan supplies and resources. Some industries have been using predictive analytics to forecast demand for many years and, with today's analytics revolution, a lot of new organizations are taking advantage of these techniques to do it.

In this chapter, we'll use a bike sharing dataset to create an application to analyze rental activity, and after this, we'll add information on demand forecasting by using Linear Regression.

We'll divide this chapter into four sections:

- Initially, we'll download and study our dataset. To explore the dataset we'll use Qlik Sense. We've previously used Rattle to explore our data, but as I've mentioned, you can explore the dataset with both tools depending on your preference. I prefer Qlik Sense for exploration. After this chapter, you'll be able to decide which tool you prefer for exploration.

- After we understand the data, we'll build a Qlik Sense application that will help users to explore the data.

- After creating the Qlik Sense application, we'll load the data into Rattle to add demand forecasting information.

- Finally, we'll add the forecast information to our Qlik Sense application.

Understanding the bike rental problem

As in other examples, we're going to use a dataset from the School of Information and Computer Science at the University of California. The dataset is taken from the location specified here:

> Bache, K. and Lichman, M. (2013). UCI Machine Learning Repository [http://archive.ics.uci.edu/ml]. Irvine, CA: University of California, School of Information and Computer Science.

In this chapter, we will use the `Bike Sharing Dataset`. You can access the dataset here https://archive.ics.uci.edu/ml/datasets/Bike+Sharing+Dataset. This dataset contains the hourly and daily count of rental bikes between the years of 2011 and 2012 in the Washington bikeshare system, with the corresponding weather and seasonal information. This dataset was originally taken from the location specified here:

> Fanaee-T, Hadi, and Gama, Joao, 'Event labeling combining ensemble detectors and background knowledge', Progress in Artificial Intelligence (2013): pp. 1-15, Springer Berlin Heidelberg.

Bike sharing systems allow people to borrow a bike from a station and return it to another station on a very short term basis.

In this bike sharing system, there are two types of users—registered and casual. **Registered** users are long-term or mid-term members of a bike sharing program. Usually, **casual** users are members of the program for just one day.

The objective is to create an application that enables control of the activity of the bike sharing system and the following week's forecast based on weather and seasonal information.

Applications that control activity are useful to different kinds of businesses. If you have information about the cost and income related to this activity, you can create an application that controls activity, costs, incomes, and margins. This application could be very useful when optimizing processes.

Demand forecasting is very common in predictive analytics. We can use different methods to forecast the demand of bike rental, but we're going to use Linear Regression. With this last example, we have now covered three main techniques—K-means for Clustering, Decision Trees, and Linear Regression.

We introduced Linear Regression in *Chapter 6, Decision Trees and Other Supervised Learning Methods*, as a method to find a statistical model that describes past data. In this way, we can use the model to predict new data.

The dataset contains two files, `day.csv` and `hour.csv`. The first file contains rental, seasonal and weather data aggregated by day. The second file contains the same data, but aggregated by hour:

- `instant`: This is the recording index
- `dteday`: This is the date
- `season`: This is the season (1: spring, 2: summer, 3: fall, 4: winter)
- `yr`: This is the year (0: 2011, 1:2012)
- `mnth`: This is the month (1 to 12)
- `hr`: This is the hour (0 to 23)
- `holiday`: This states whether the day is a holiday or not

  Source: `http://dchr.dc.gov/page/holiday-schedule`

- `weekday`: The day of the week
- `workingday`: If the day is neither a weekend nor a holiday, then it is 1, otherwise it is 0
- `weathersit`: This provides the following four options:
    - 1: Clear, Few clouds, Partly cloudy
    - 2: Mist + Cloudy, Mist + Broken clouds, Mist + Few clouds, Mist
    - 3: Light Snow, Light Rain + Thunderstorm + Scattered clouds, Light Rain + Scattered clouds
    - 4: Heavy Rain + Ice Pallets + Thunderstorm + Mist, Snow + Fog
- `temp`: The normalized temperature in Celsius, the values are divided by 41 (max)
- `atemp`: The normalized feeling temperature in Celsius, the values are divided by 50 (max)
- `hum`: The normalized humidity, the values are divided by 100 (max)
- `windspeed`: The normalized wind speed, the values are divided by 67 (max)
- `casual`: The count of casual users
- `registered`: The count of registered users
- `cnt`: The count of total rental bikes, including both casual and registered

This dataset has three dependent variables, casual, registered and cnt; 13 independent variables, dteday, season, yr, mnth, hr, holiday, weekday, workingday, weathersit, temp, atemp, hum and windspeed, and one identity variable, instant.

If we can find the relationship between the weather variables and the number of users, we'll be able to predict the demand using a weather forecast.

For this example, we're going to use the daily file and the dependent variable cnt. We're going to ignore the hourly information and registered and casual variables.

In order to add some context to our analysis, we will assume a target of 4,000 users per day. We have the same capacity (the number of bikes) every day, so on the days with less than 4,000 users, we are wasting our capacity.

Exploring the data with Qlik Sense

We've seen in previous chapters how to load data into Qlik Sense and how to create charts. In this chapter, we'll discuss different charts, but we're not going to describe how to load the data and how to create charts. In this section, we will build a Qlik Sense application using the data contained in the day.csv file. Before starting to build the application, we will explore it.

Checking for temporal patterns

We can start creating a chart to see the evolution of the number of rentals, as shown in the following screenshot. We've used a bar chart with the variable dteday as **Dimension** and sum(cnt), the total number of users, as **Measure**:

In the bar chart, we usually use the measure to order the bars. If we use a bar chart to see the sales performance of different countries, we will have to order based on the amount of sales. In this case, I will have to order the bars by the dteday dimension. To ensure I'm using this variable to order my bar chart, I need to check the sorting order. As you can see in the following screenshot, I set dteday as the first variable to sort the data:

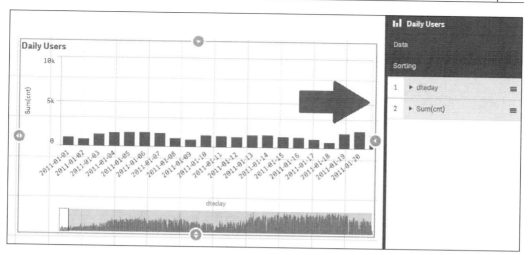

Looking at the following chart, we discover that on 29th October 2012, there was an unusually low number of rentals; on that day the system reports only 22 rentals. The reason for this unusual behavior is that on 29th October 2012, and 30th October, 2012, Hurricane Sandy hit Washington DC. We'll delete these two days from our dataset, before loading it into Rattle to avoid anomalies:

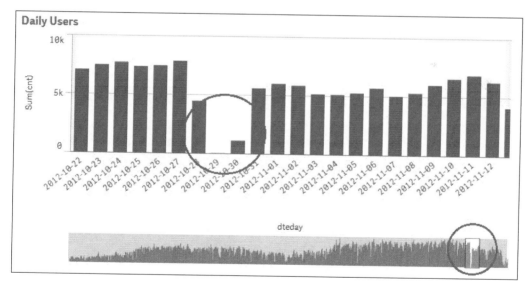

In the previous chart, we can also see that, in 2012, the bike rental increased, compared to 2011. We can replace the dimension `dteday` by `yr` to see the difference between 2011 (`yr = 0`) and 2012 (`yr = 1`). As you can see in the following screenshot, in 2011 the number of users was 1.243.103 and in 2012 the number was 2.049.576:

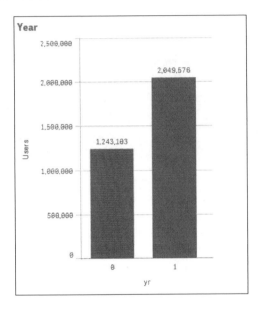

In the next chart, we'll use the average number of rental users and the weekday as the dimension to discover a behavior pattern for weekdays:

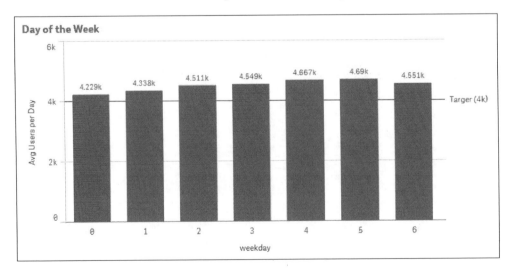

Looking at the preceding chart, we can see that the day of the week has a weak influence on the number of users. During the weekend, the average number of users is slightly lower.

As you can see, I've added the target to the chart. You learned in the previous chapter how to add reference lines to our charts.

In the following screenshot, you can see the relation between the variables `mnth` and `season` and the dependent variables `registered` and `casual`:

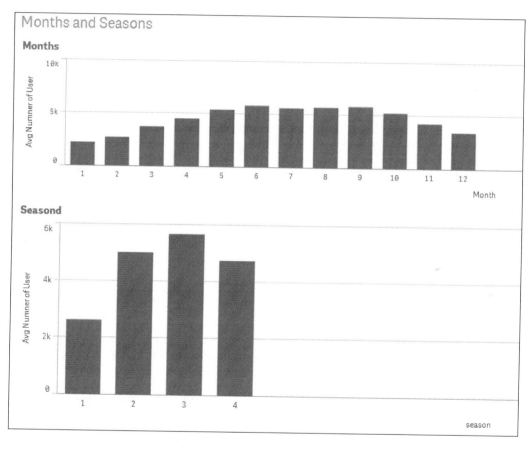

As you can see, there is a relationship between the month and the number of rentals. During the cooler months of January, December and February, demand is at its lowest and, during the warmer months of July, August and September, demand is higher. But, is it a linear relationship?

A regression model assumes a lineal relationship between the independent variable and the dependent variable. Usually, the relationship between the size of a house and its price is lineal; a big house has a higher price than a small house.

January (month 1) and December (month 12) have a smaller number of registered users than July (month 7). The relationship between the month, season, and the dependent variable is not lineal. We'll transform these variables later.

There is also a relationship between `workingday`, `holiday` and the dependent variables. Create the charts to check it.

Visual correlation analysis

We can use Rattle for correlation analysis, but we can also use Qlik Sense to do a very intuitive correlation analysis.

Karl Pover wrote a very interesting chapter on *Learning QlikView Data Visualization, Packt Publishing*, about how to use scatter plots for correlation analysis.

Create a scatter plot using `dteday` as the dimension and `temp` and `atemp` as measures, and you will get a chart similar to the following screenshot:

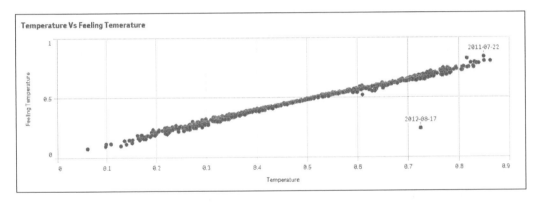

This chart shows us the relationship between temperature and feeling temperature. Of course, there is a strong relationship between the two variables.

Now, we will use a scatter plot and a bar chart to explore the correlation between temperature, wind speed, humidity, and the total number of users, as shown in the following screenshot. We will start with the variable temperature:

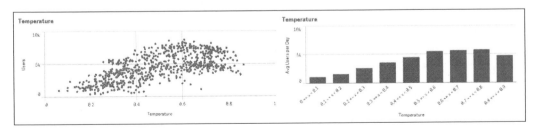

The left chart is a scatter plot much like the previous screenshot; each point is a different day, and we can clearly see that there is a strong relationship between temperature and the number of users. Users prefer warm days.

The chart on the right-hand side helps us to better understand the relationship between temperature and the average number of users. The measure of the chart is the average number of users, and the dimension is the range of the temperature. To create this dimension, I used the function class, as shown in this screenshot:

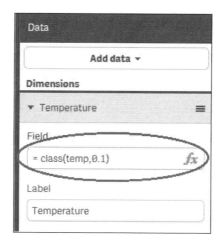

The class function creates the different ranges and the second parameter (0.1) is the width of every class.

Now, repeat these two charts for the variables hum and windspeed. You will discover that the relationships between humidity, wind speed, and the number of users are weaker than the previously used variables, as shown in this screenshot:.

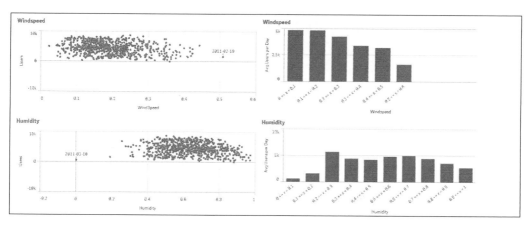

We've used Qlik Sense to explore and understand the data, and we've discovered that there is a strong relationship between the number of total users and the temperature. During the warmest months, the number of users increases, and during the coldest months, the number of users decreases. Now, we'll create an app to help users analyze the demand.

Creating a Qlik Sense App to control the activity

In the previous chapter, we explored the DAR approach to develop Qlik Sense applications; in this section, we will use the same approach.

We'll start with the dashboard. At the center, we'll place the most important information or measures. The most important details are the average number of users and the total number of users; these KPIs will occupy the main area of our application. The number of registered and casual users is also important, and we'll keep space for them in the dashboard, as shown here:

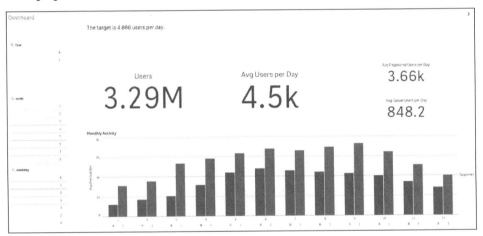

During our analysis, we discovered that, in 2012, the number of users increased, and that, during the colder months, we had a lack of activity. I've used a bar chart to show you the difference between 2011 and 2012 and the lack of activity during the winter.

After the dashboard, you will need an analysis sheet to analyze the months that have a lack of activity. In this analysis sheet, we'll include charts with just two metrics—the average number of users and the total number of users; we'll combine these metrics with the most important dimensions. The user will be able to see the same problem from different points of view and make selections in the charts to see the effect in the other dimensions.

In the previous section, we discovered that the variable that has a greater influence on the activity is temperature. For this reason, I decided to use color to add this measure in all charts.

In the central row, you can see the relationship between the activity and the humidity, and the wind speed and temperature. Using the color to add the temperature to the charts, the users will keep focused on this colored variable, as shown in this screenshot:

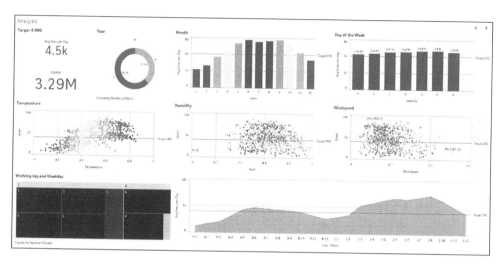

In this analysis sheet, the user can use the chart as a filter. Go to the temperature scatter plot and choose the days that have under 4,000 users, as shown in the following screenshot. After analyzing low performing days, you will have discovered that the days of the week with the worst performance is Saturday.

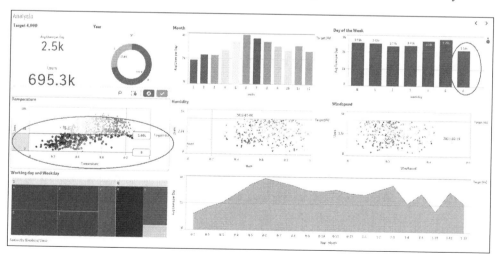

Use the month chart to filter January, February, and March, and you will see that, during these months, Saturday and Sunday the are days with very low performance. Perhaps we can plan a promotional activity during these days to improve our activity level.

Finally, in our reporting sheet, we can place one or more tables to be able to see detailed information about the activity each day.

Using Rattle to forecast the demand

In this section, we'll use Rattle for a quick correlation analysis and to create a model to forecast the bike demand.

Correlation Analysis with Rattle

Our dataset has three possible target variables: cnt, registered, and casual. Rattle doesn't handle multiple targets. We can create a model for registered and a second model for casual and add both values to have the total number of users, or we can build a model for cnt (the total amount). We will only create a model for cnt because we're interested in the level of activity and this variable will provide it.

Load the dataset into Rattle and set instant to Ident and dteday, registered and casual to Ignore, and set the rest of variables to Input.

To perform the correlation analysis, go to the **Explore** tab, select the **Correlation** radio button and, finally, press the **Execute** button, as shown in this screenshot:

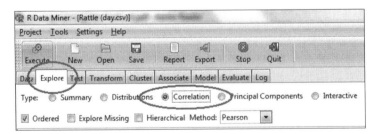

Rattle will return us a correlation matrix and a correlation plot. The correlation matrix is a matrix that displays the correlations between variables. In the following screenshot, you can see a reduced correlation matrix. We've ignored some variables to create a simple version of the correlation matrix. The correlation index is a number between -1 and 1. When the coefficient is 1, the variables are perfectly correlated. If the coefficient is -1, the variables are perfectly and negatively related. If the coefficient is 0, the variables are not related and are not useful when predicting a new value. In order to describe the different correlation coefficients, we can use these rules:

- greater than `0.7`: A very strong positive relationship
- `0.4` to `0.7`: A strong positive relationship
- `0.3` to `0.4`: A moderate positive relationship
- `0.2` to `0.3`: A weak positive relationship
- `0.2` to `-0.2`: A negligible relationship
- `-0.2` to `-0.3`: A weak negative relationship
- `-0.3` to `-0.4`: A moderate negative relationship
- `-0.4` to `-0.7`: A strong negative relationship
- less than `-0.7`: A very strong negative relationship

The following screenshot shows the correlation summary:

```
Correlation summary using the 'Pearson' covariance.

Note that only correlations between numeric variables are reported.

                windspeed       holiday    workingday          weekday     weathersit
windspeed     1.000000000  -0.002138282  -0.001560627    0.0072097243    0.019696893
holiday      -0.002138282   1.000000000  -0.265080924   -0.1167294529   -0.035618710
workingday   -0.001560627  -0.265080924   1.000000000    0.0409517959    0.036544724
weekday       0.007209724  -0.116729453   0.040951796    1.0000000000    0.018991914
weathersit    0.019696893  -0.035618710   0.036544724    0.0189919137    1.000000000
yr           -0.026605114   0.001759249   0.022853155   -0.0007176284   -0.031865947
hum          -0.249789799  -0.019085193  -0.022536858   -0.0421432549    0.635618502
temp         -0.129407940  -0.042122706   0.059877976    0.0277297718   -0.098747332
atemp        -0.157154074  -0.047527991   0.057232999    0.0236027677   -0.094983995
cnt          -0.232535932  -0.083692129   0.095895392    0.1040646910   -0.288818791
mnth         -0.205734775   0.019274288  -0.010169220    0.0073114706    0.041825772
season       -0.206270773  -0.024476785  -0.001246263    0.0030517333    0.007360641
                       yr           hum          temp          atemp            cnt
windspeed    -0.0266051144  -0.24978980   -0.12940794   -0.15715407   -0.23253593
holiday       0.0017592489  -0.01908519    0.04212271   -0.04752799   -0.08369213
workingday    0.0228531545  -0.02253686    0.05987798    0.05723300    0.09589539
weekday      -0.0007176284  -0.04214325    0.02772977    0.02360277    0.10406469
weathersit   -0.0318659473   0.63561850   -0.09874733   -0.09498399   -0.28881879
yr            1.0000000000  -0.11515648    0.05666152    0.05191096    0.57115393
hum          -0.1151564848   1.00000000    0.11056228    0.12845472   -0.13944589
temp          0.0566615209   0.11056228    1.00000000    0.98977296    0.63082829
atemp         0.0519109640   0.12845472    0.98977296    1.00000000    0.63077395
cnt           0.5711539293  -0.13944589    0.63082829    0.63077395    1.00000000
mnth          0.0292674143   0.21963639    0.23059473    0.23885273    0.30162668
season        0.0410655502   0.17984302    0.33149921    0.34015894    0.42383148
                     mnth        season
windspeed    -0.205734775  -0.206270773
holiday       0.019274288  -0.024476785
workingday   -0.010169220  -0.001246263
weekday       0.007311471   0.003051733
weathersit    0.041825772   0.007360641
yr            0.029267414   0.041065550
hum           0.219636389   0.179843016
temp          0.230594733   0.331499211
atemp         0.238852732   0.340158943
cnt           0.301626677   0.423831483
mnth          1.000000000   0.829079430
season        0.829079430   1.000000000

Rattle timestamp: 2015-06-25 02:53:38
====================================================================
```

Notice that there is a strong correlation between **temp** (temperature) and **atemp** (feeling temperature) and that our target variable **cnt** has a strong correlation with variables **temp**, **atemp**, and **yr**. We already knew this because we discovered that the correlation helps explore the dataset with Qlik Sense.

In the following screenshot, we can see the correlation plot. The color and size of the ball explains the predictive power of each variable. For the dependent variable **cnt**, the independent variables, **yr**, **atemp**, **temp**, and **season**, are strong predictors. The independent variable **mnth** is a moderate predictor. Finally, **windspeed** and **weathersit**, are weak predictors:

 Please note that you need to tick **Verbose**, and **Advanced Graphics** in the **Settings** menu to generate the following screenshot. The ticking of **Use Cairo Graphics Device** is optional. Also note that the inner Rattle window **R Data Miner - [Rattle]**, should not be maximized because the generated screenshot tends to go behind the current window.

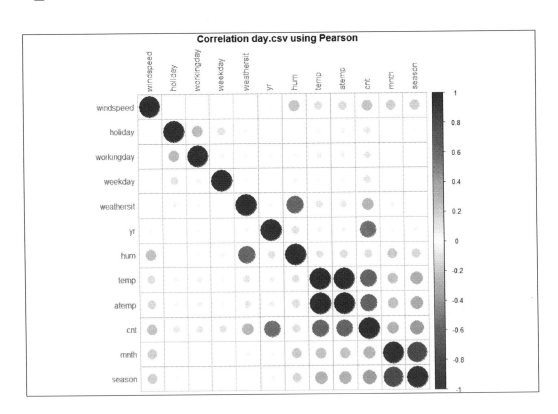

As we've seen in Qlik Sense, variables `temp` and `atemp` have a strong correlation. We will use just one of them; for this reason, we will set `atemp` to `Ignore`.

Building a model

Creating a predictive model is an iterative process; we start by creating a model with the training dataset. Then we evaluate the performance with the validation dataset, and we modify the model and create a new model. Finally, when we feel comfortable, we can test the performance of our model with the testing dataset.

In this example, we won't tune the performance of the model.

Go to the **Data** tab and set `cnt` to **target** and `atemp` to **Ignore**. To create the model, go to the **Model** tab, select the **Linear** radio button and press **Execute**, as shown in the following screenshot:

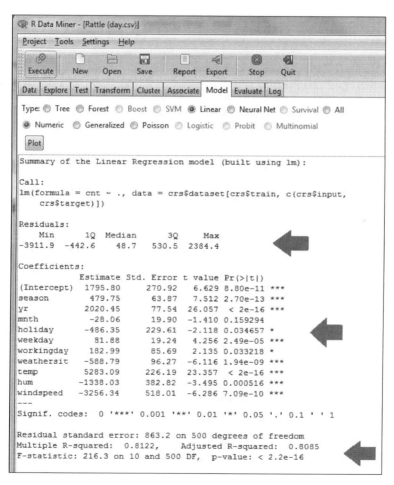

After the execution, examine the summary report provided by Rattle, starting with the **Residuals** section. The maximum error is **2384.4** and the minimum is **-3911.9**. This error looks very high. Notice that 50 percent of the occurrences are between the first and the third quartile, so 50 percent of the time our error of trying to estimate users is between -**442.6** and **530.5**.

In the coefficients section, the last column shows us the significance of each variable or the predictive power— *** for strong predictive power and * for weak predictive power.

The last section, Adjusted R-squared, explains how accurate our model is when predicting the values of the dependent variable. In our example, the value of R-squared is **0.8122**, which means that 81.22 percent of the variation of cnt is explained by our model.

To have a reference of the model performance, we need to test its predictive power against the validation dataset. As we saw in *Chapter 7, Model Evaluation*, to evaluate the performance of a regression model, we can use a plot called Predicted versus Observed Plot (**Pr v Ob**), as shown here:

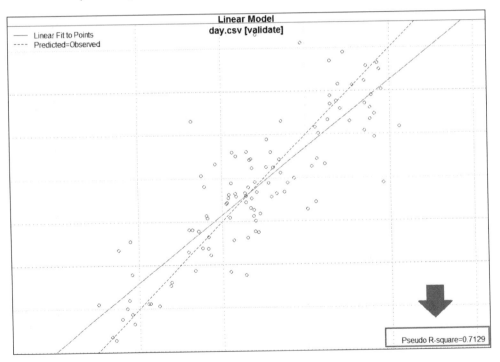

We've created a model that has **Pseuso R-square = 0.7129**. In the next section, we'll try to improve the performance of the model by transforming numeric variables with a non-lineal relationship with the dependent variables.

Improving performance

Now, we will enter in an iterative process, tune the model, and check the performance with the validation dataset until we achieve the performance needed. We will see how to make a transformation with an example. In this section, we will only make a small transformation.

As we've seen in the previous section, we have numeric variables that have a non-lineal relationship with the target variable.

To explain how to transform the variables, we're going to use the variable, season. As we've seen, season is a numeric variable that has a non-lineal relationship with registered. We would like to transform the numeric variable with four different values to four flags or indicators, as shown in the following table:

Season	Spring flag	Summer flag	Fall flag	Winter flag
1	1	0	0	0
2	0	1	0	0
3	0	0	1	0
4	0	0	0	1

We're going to transform the variable in two different steps. Go to the **Transform** tab, select the variable, **season**, select the **Recode** radio button, select the **As Categoric** radio button and press **Execute**, as shown in the following screenshot:

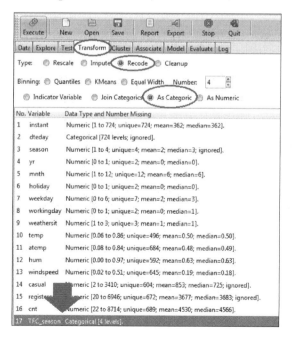

Rattle has added a new variable called **TFC_season**; this is a categorical variable. For the second step, go to the **Transform** tab, select the variable **TFC_season**, select the **Recode** Radio button, select the **Indicator Variable** Radio button and press **Execute**. After these operations are done, you will see the following result:

16	cnt	Numeric [22 to 8714; unique=696; mean=4504; median=4548].
17	TFC_season	Categorical [4 levels; ignored].
18	TIN_TFC_season_.1.1.	Numeric [0.00 to 1.00; unique=2; mean=0.25; median=0.00].
19	TIN_TFC_season_.1.2.	Numeric [0.00 to 1.00; unique=2; mean=0.25; median=0.00].
20	TIN_TFC_season_.2.3.	Numeric [0.00 to 1.00; unique=2; mean=0.26; median=0.00].
21	TIN_TFC_season_.3.4.	Numeric [0.00 to 1.00; unique=2; mean=0.24; median=0.00].

Remapped variables added to the dataset with 'TIN_' prefix.

Now Rattle has created four new numeric variables. Each variable has two possible values, 0 or 1.

You need to create the model again but, before that, ensure that the new flag variables are selected as input, as shown in this screenshot:

17	TFC_season	Categoric	⊙	⊙	⊙	⊙	◉	⊙	Unique: 4
18	TIN_TFC_season_.1.1.	Numeric	◉	⊙	⊙	⊙	⊙	⊙	Unique: 2
19	TIN_TFC_season_.1.2.	Numeric	◉	⊙	⊙	⊙	⊙	⊙	Unique: 2
20	TIN_TFC_season_.2.3.	Numeric	◉	⊙	⊙	⊙	⊙	⊙	Unique: 2
21	TIN_TFC_season_.3.4.	Numeric	◉	⊙	⊙	⊙	⊙	⊙	Unique: 2

After creating the new model, review the new R-squared and Adjusted R-squared values and you will see some improvement in performance.

As we've explained before, the process of improving or tuning a model is iterative. After the performance evaluation, you can transform your data or modify the model and evaluate the performance again until your performance is acceptable.

Model evaluation

As we saw in *Chapter 7, Model Evaluation*, to evaluate the performance of a regression model, we can use a plot called Predicted versus Observed Plot (**Pr v Ob**), as shown here:

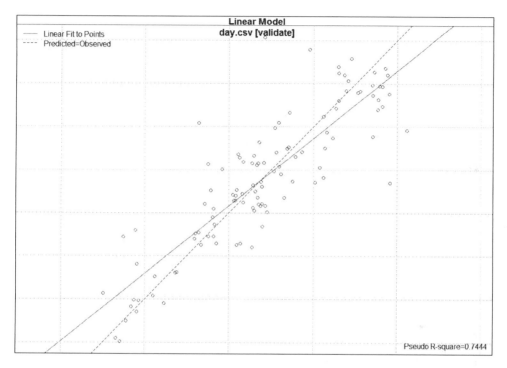

We've quickly developed a model that achieved a Pseudo R-square of **0.744**. We did a small optimization in the model; we can improve the performance by working with the different variables.

After improving the model using the training dataset to build the model and the validation dataset to evaluate this performance, we need to confirm the performance of our model by creating a Predicted versus Observed Plot with the test dataset. We can do that to detect overfitting.

A very interesting feature of Rattle is that we can run multiple models and evaluate the performance of the different models. Go to the **Model** tab and build a Neural Network model. Now, return to the **Evaluate** tab and select the **Linear** and **Neural Net** checkboxes and press the **Execute** button, you can compare the two different models, as shown in the following screenshot. As we saw in *Chapter 6, Decision Trees and Other Supervised Learning Methods*, Neural Networks are a kind of algorithm inspired by biological Neural Networks which are used to approximate functions:

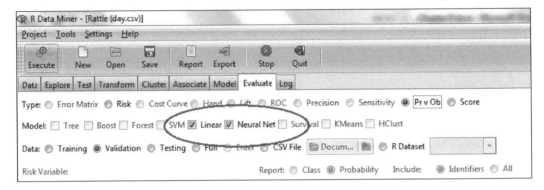

Now that we have a model to predict the demand of rental bikes, we want to add demand forecast information to our Qlik Sense application.

The first step is to predict the new values, or forecast the demand. The second and final step is to load the data into Qlik Sense.

Scoring new data

We have three main options to score new data, these are listed as follows:

- **Qlik Sense**:
    - We've found the coefficients for the regression; we can use it in Qlik Sense during the data loading or we can create a measure with the formula.
    - This option has a great disadvantage; we would normally prefer to re-evaluate the model with new data. If we change the model, we will have to update the Qlik Sense app.
- **R**:
    - We can save our model in Rattle and then we can load the model in R.
    - We can use the predict() function to score new data. This is a good option but the last option is the easiest of all.

- **Rattle**:

    ○ In Rattle's **Evaluate** tab, we can use the Score option. Using this option, we can score the training, the validation or the testing dataset, or we can load a dataset from a CSV file.

In a real case, we will have the weather forecast for the next week, and we'll use Rattle to load the data from a CSV file. In this example, we don't have next week's forecast and we'll score the testing dataset and the complete dataset.

Go to the **Evaluate** tab, select **Score**, **Testing**, and **All** and press the **Execute** button. Rattle will score the testing dataset for you and will write the prediction in a CSV file. This file will include all original variables and a new variable called `glm` with the predicted value, as shown in the following screenshot. Before finishing, you need to confirm the location and name of the file:

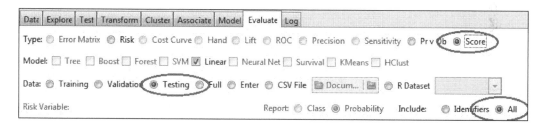

Now, we will check the performance of our model by using Qlik Sense. Create a new Qlik Sense application and load the file generated by Rattle. This file contains `111` rows and the testing dataset, and each row contains all the original data and the predicted value. Create a scatter plot with `dteday` as the dimension and `glm` and `cnt` as measures, as shown here:

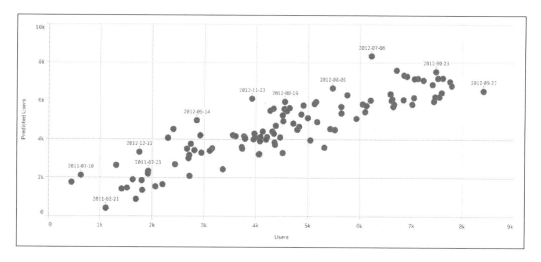

We've created a Predicted versus Observed Plot with the testing dataset. This chart and the one we created in Rattle gives us an idea of the predictive power of our model. We don't need this plot because we've created it in Rattle.

Now, come back to Rattle to score the complete dataset. Select the **Full** dataset and report just the **Identifiers** included, as shown here:

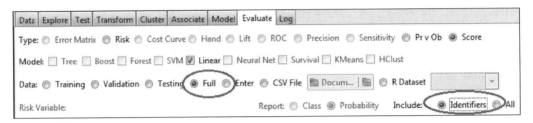

Rattle will create a file with 731 observation with all the original columns and a new column with the predicted value called glm.

We will load this information in to our original bikes application. Go to Qlik Sense, open the original application, and drag and drop this second file into the application. Qlik Sense will ask you if you want to add new data or replace the current data, if yes, then select **Add data**. After loading the data, open **Data model viewer**, as shown in the following screenshot:

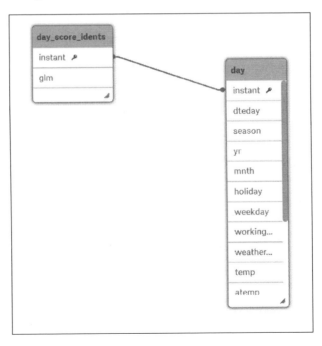

Rattle has created a file that contains variables, the identifier **ident** and the prediction **glm**. When we load this file into Qlik Sense, it creates an association with our original table using the field **ident**. Finally, create two charts to show the predictive power of our model. In the first chart, I used a line chart with **dteday** as the dimension and **cnt** and **glm** as measures, as shown here:

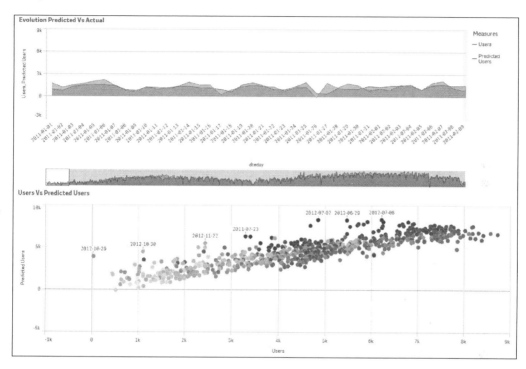

Be careful with these plots, we've added the training dataset and the validation and testing ones. We used training and validation datasets to build the model, so this plot doesn't provide us a real idea of the predictive power of our model. The previous plots we did just with the testing dataset gave us a real idea of the performance.

In the real world, we will load the weather forecast for the following week into Rattle and we will score it. By loading historic and forecast data into Qlik Sense, we will be able to create visualizations that are similar to the following screenshot, which shows historic and forecast data together:

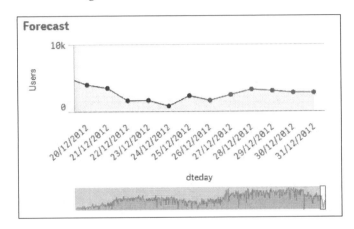

Further learning

Predictive Analytics and Data Visualizations are huge topics and in this book I just introduced the key concepts.

Related to Qlik Sense, we forget a lot of important things. In my opinion, the data load editor is among the most powerful. In order to learn more about Qlik Sense and the **Data load editor**, you may want to check out:

Learning Qlik® Sense: The Official Guide, Christopher Ilacqua, Henric Cronström, James Richardson. Packt Publishing.

In order to increase your knowledge and learn more about Qlik Sence, I suggested you some books and web sites. A very good source of information and advice can be the Qlik Community:

`https://community.qlik.com`

This is the most active community in the BI landscape.

You also learned how to use Rattle to create predictive models. In this book, we've focused on Clustering, Decision Trees, and Linear Regression; these are the most common predictive techniques. You can use these techniques in your own datasets to provide insights. To improve your Rattle knowledge, the best book is *Data Mining with Rattle and R, The Art of Excavating Data for Knowledge Discovery, Graham Williams, Springer.*

The videos listed on this page are also a good source of knowledge:

```
http://rattle.togaware.com/rattle-videos.html
```

Rattle also has a very interesting users group:

```
https://groups.google.com/forum/#!forum/rattle-users
```

Finally, if you prefer to learn predictive techniques with R, try *Machine Learning with R, Brett Lantz, Packt Publishing*.

A funny and very good way to improve your skills in predictive analytics is Kaggle. This is the world's largest community of data scientists. In this community, you can find *data science* competitions. We've not used the term data science in this book; there are a lot of new terms around analytics, and we tried to focus on just a few to avoid confusion. Currently, we use this term to refer to an engineering area dedicated to collecting, cleaning, and manipulating data to unearth new knowledge. At www.kaggle.com, you can find different types of competitions. There are introductory competitions for beginners, and there are competitions with monetary prizes. You can access a competition, download the data and the problem description, and create your own solutions. An example of a Kaggle competition is the bike sharing example we used in this chapter.

Finally, in *Chapter 1*, *Getting Ready with Predictive Analytics*, we introduced *Competing on Analytics*, by Thomas H. Davenport and Jeanne G Harris, *Harvard Business Review Press*; if you are worried about how to apply predictive analytics at a business level, start with this book.

Summary

In this chapter, we used Qlik Sense to explore the bike sharing dataset. In Qlik Sense, we saw different ways of doing an intuitive correlation analysis.

After this, we created an application to analyze the rental activity. The application had three sheets following the DAR approach.

Finally, we used Rattle to confirm the correlation analysis we did with Qlik Sense, then we created a predictive model to forecast the demand depending on the weather forecast.

With Rattle, we used the variable `cnt` as the target variable; it would be very interesting to repeat the exercise using the variables `registered` and `casual`.

You've arrived at the end of the book, so by now you should understand the basics of predictive analytics and data visualization and have gained some expertise in using Rattle and Qlik Sense Desktop.

Now you can use Qlik Sense to quickly analyze business data. With Qlik Sense you can discover hidden patterns in your data and create powerful visualizations to present the conclusions of your analysis.

Index

Text & image 162
Treemap 162
dendrogram 106
descriptive analytics 92
disadvantages, Decision Tree Learning
overfitting 114
unstable 114
distributions
categorical variables 51
numeric variables 46
visualizing 46

E

Ensemble methods
about 134
boosting 135-137
Random Forest 138-140
Supported Vector Machine (SVM) 141
URL 134
entropy 114-120
environment
installing 7
error rate 151
Exploratory Data Analysis (EDA) 39
Explore Missing option 57

F

fact table 175

G

General Public License (GNU) 5
Graphical User Interface (GUI) 5

H

hierarchical clustering 104-106
Hierarchical option 57

I

indicator variables
about 35
As Category option 36
As Numeric option 36
Join Categories option 36

information gain 114-120
input variables 21

K

Kaggle
about 20
URL 20
Key Performance Indicator (KPI) 159, 173
K-means 91
kurtosis
about 42
URL 43

L

labeled dataset 92
Logistic Regression 142, 143
Lower Confidence Level 44

M

Machine Learning (ML)
about 91
association analysis 107-109
cluster analysis 93
hierarchical clustering 104-106
supervised learning 92
unsupervised learning 92
measures of central tendency
mean 40
median 40
mode 40
measures of dispersion
about 41
quartiles 41
range 41
standard deviation 42
variance 42
menus, charts
Add-ons menu 170
Appearance menu 171, 172
Data menu 166-169
Sorting menu 169
model evaluation
about 209
new data, scoring 210-213
performing 209, 210

Risk Chart
  about 154
  obtaining 154-156
ROC Curve 156, 157
roles, variable
  ident 22
  identifier 22
  Ignore 22
  input 22
  risk 22
  target 22
R-Square 148

S

simple data app
  creating 68
Simple Linear Regression 143
skewness
  about 42
  URL 43
standard deviation 42
Standard Error 44
summary reports
  about 40
  measures of central tendency 40
  measures of dispersion 41
  measures of shape of distribution 42
supervised learning 92
Supported Vector Machine (SVM) 141

T

target variables 21
testing 145

text summaries
  about 40
  missing values, displaying 44, 45
  summary reports 40
training dataset 92
types of predictions, classifiers performance
  False Negative 149
  False Positive 149
  True Negative 149
  True Positive 149

U

UCI Machine Learning Repository
  reference 147
underfitting 120, 121
unlabeled dataset 92, 107
unsupervised learning 92
Upper Confidence Level 44
user groups
  analysts 173
  executive management 173
  middle managers 173

V

validation 145
variable 22
variance 42
visualization toolbox 160

W

Weka 22